LSAT®
PrepTest 79
Unlocked

Exclusive Data, Analysis & Explanations for the
September 2016 LSAT

KAPLAN

PUBLISHING

New York

LSAT® is a registered mark of the Law School Admission Council, Inc.

© 2017 by Kaplan, Inc.

Published by Kaplan Publishing, a division of Kaplan, Inc.
750 Third Avenue
New York, NY 10017

ISBN: 978-1-5062-2337-7
10 9 8 7 6 5 4 3 2 1

The Inside Story

PrepTest 79 was administered in September 2016. It challenged 33,563 test takers. What made this test so hard? Here's a breakdown of what Kaplan students who were surveyed after taking the official exam considered PrepTest 79's most difficult section.

Hardest PrepTest 79 Section as Reported by Test Takers

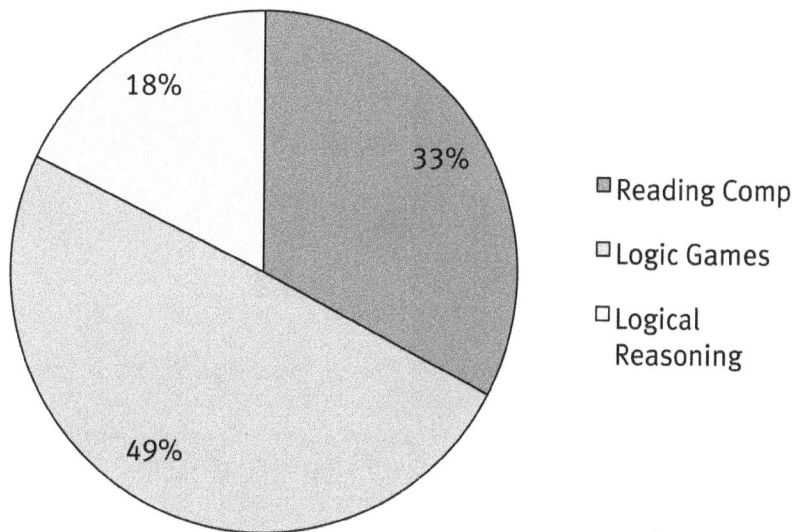

18%

33%

49%

▣ Reading Comp

▫ Logic Games

▫ Logical Reasoning

Based on these results, you might think that studying Logic Games is the key to LSAT success. Well, Logic Games is important, but test takers' perceptions don't tell the whole story. For that, you need to consider students' actual performance. The following chart shows the average number of students to miss each question in each of PrepTest 79's different sections.

Percentage Incorrect By PrepTest 79 Section Type

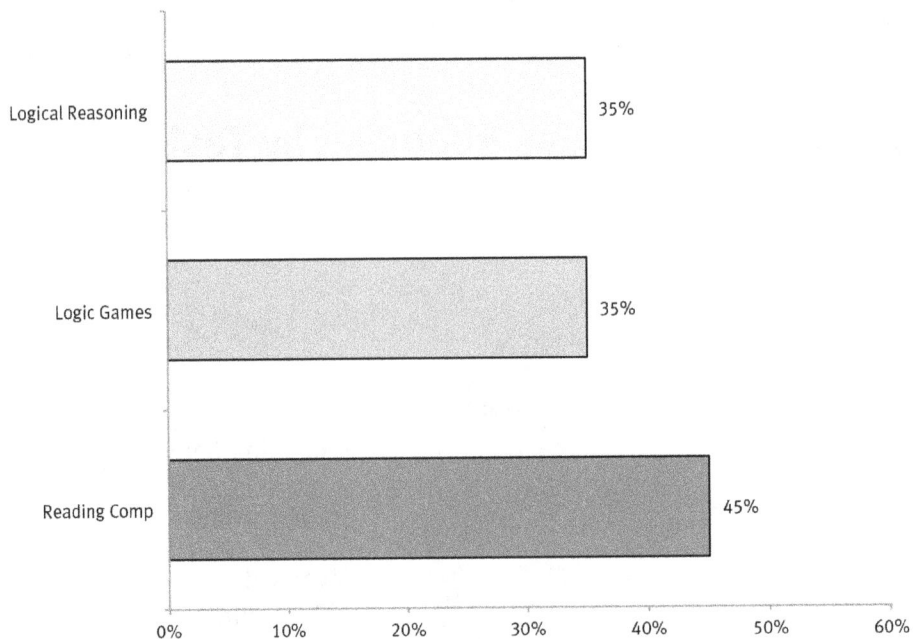

Section	Percentage
Logical Reasoning	35%
Logic Games	35%
Reading Comp	45%

0% 10% 20% 30% 40% 50% 60%

Maybe students overestimate the difficulty of the Logic Games section because it's so unusual, or maybe it's because a really hard Logic Game is so easy to remember after the test. But the truth is that the test maker places hard questions throughout the test. Here were the locations of the 10 hardest (most missed) questions in the exam.

Location of 10 Most Difficult Questions in PrepTest 79

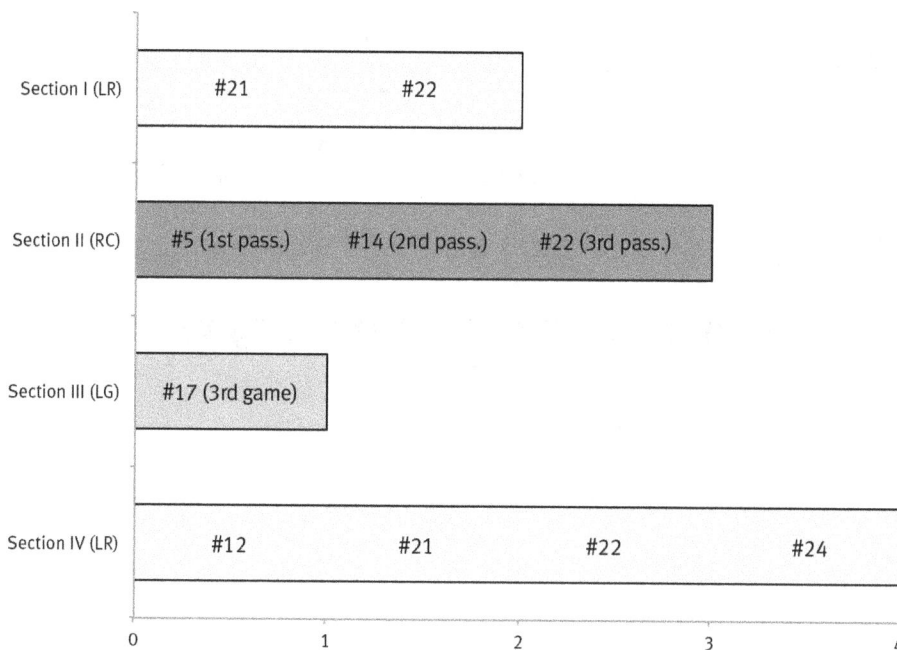

The takeaway from this data is that, to maximize your potential on the LSAT, you need to take a comprehensive approach. Test yourself rigorously, and review your performance on every section of the test. Kaplan's LSAT explanations provide the expertise and insight you need to fully understand your results. The explanations are written and edited by a team of LSAT experts, who have helped thousands of students improve their scores. Kaplan always provides data-driven analysis of the test, ranking the difficulty of every question based on actual student performance. The ten hardest questions on every test are highlighted with a 4-star difficulty rating, the highest we give. The analysis breaks down the remaining questions into 1-, 2-, and 3-star ratings so that you can compare your performance to thousands of other test takers on all LSAC material.

Don't settle for wondering whether a question was really as hard as it seemed to you. Analyze the test with real data, and learn the secrets and strategies that help top scorers master the LSAT.

7 Can't–Miss Features of PrepTest 79

- With 10 Assumption questions, PrepTest 79 was only the second test since September '09 (PT 58) with 10 or more.
- Although there were two Parallel Flaw questions, PrepTest 79 was only the second test *ever* with no Parallel Reasoning questions. The other time was in September '09 (PT 58).
- PrepTest 79 featured two Distribution games—which was only the fourth time that had ever happened on a released test, as of the time of PT 79's release.
- Although Loose Sequencing game sketches feature branches to indicate relative relationships, Game 4 on PrepTest 79 was a *Strict* Sequencing game that featured a first-of-its-kind twist where the strict sequence branched. Check out the explanations for this game that was the talk of the test.
- ›Many students have reservations about the Natural Science passage. Complex language in biology, chemistry, and physics passages may be difficult for some test takers. However, the topic of the Natural Science passage on PrepTest 79 is: bodybuilding! Hanz and Franz approve!
- (C)eize the day! If you had to guess on the last question of each section, but you always selected answer choice (C), you got three of the four right!

- LSAC never reveals when its questions were written, but Question 20 of the first Logical Reasoning section showed up at a time when public debate included its subject matter on an almost daily basis leading up to the 2016 U.S. presidential election.

PrepTest 79 in Context

As much fun as it is to find out what makes a PrepTest unique or noteworthy, it's even more important to know just how representative it is of other LSAT administrations (and, thus, how likely it is to be representative of the exam you will face on Test Day). The following charts compare the numbers of each kind of question and game on PrepTest 79 to the average numbers seen on all officially released LSATs administered over the past five years (from 2012 through 2016).

Number of LR Questions by Type: PrepTest 79 vs. 2012–2016 Average

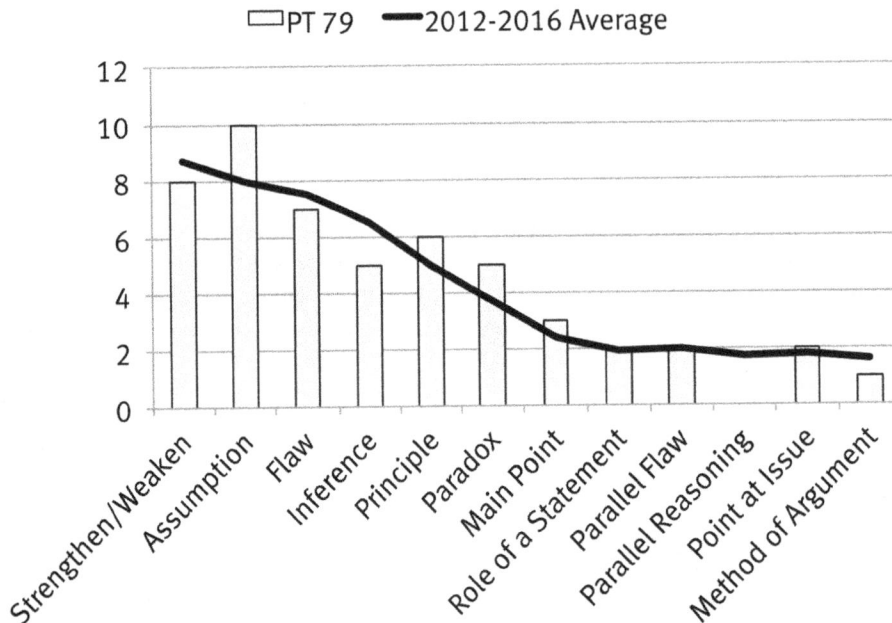

Number of LG Games by Type: PrepTest 79 vs. 2012–2016 Average

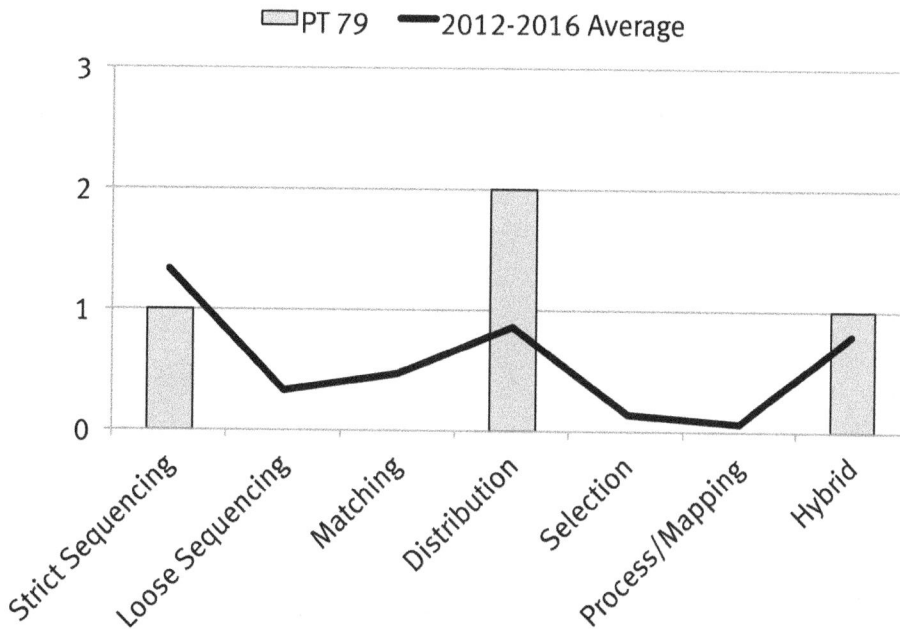

Number of RC Questions by Type: PrepTest 79 vs. 2012–2016 Average

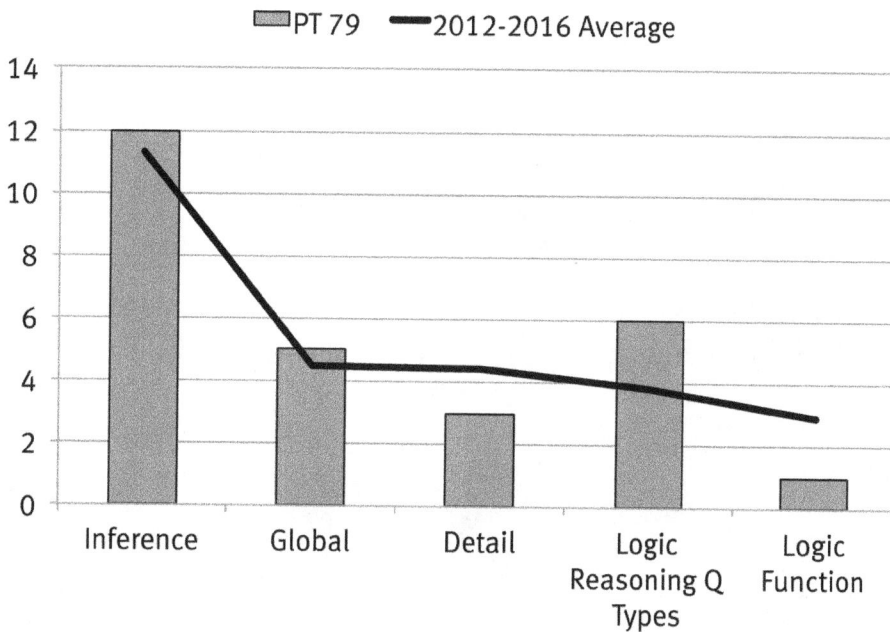

There isn't usually a huge difference in the distribution of questions from LSAT to LSAT, but if this test seems harder (or easier) to you than another you've taken, compare the number of questions of the types on which you, personally, are strongest and weakest. And then, explore within each section to see if your best or worst question types came earlier or later.

Students in Kaplan's comprehensive LSAT courses have access to every released LSAT and to an online question bank with thousands of officially released questions, games, and passages. If you are studying on your own, you have to do a bit more work to identify your strengths and your areas of opportunity. Quantitative analysis (like that in the charts above) is an important tool for understanding how the test is constructed and how you are performing on it.

KAPLAN

Section I: Logical Reasoning

Q#	Question Type	Correct	Difficulty
1	Paradox	C	★
2	Flaw	E	★
3	Paradox	D	★
4	Assumption (Necessary)	D	★
5	Paradox	B	★
6	Flaw	B	★
7	Assumption (Necessary)	A	★
8	Inference	E	★
9	Main Point	B	★
10	Strengthen	C	★★
11	Point at Issue	C	★
12	Strengthen	A	★
13	Flaw	E	★★
14	Principle (Identify/Strengthen)	E	★
15	Flaw	A	★
16	Principle (Parallel)	B	★
17	Strengthen/Weaken (Evaluate the Argument)	C	★★
18	Assumption (Necessary)	A	★★★
19	Principle (Identify/Strengthen)	D	★★★
20	Inference (EXCEPT)	D	★★★
21	Weaken	E	★★★★
22	Role of a Statement	E	★★★★
23	Strengthen	D	★★★
24	Assumption (Necessary)	B	★★
25	Inference	A	★★
26	Parallel Flaw	E	★★★

1. (C) Paradox

Step 1: Identify the Question Type

The question asks for something that "helps to resolve the apparent discrepancy," making this a Paradox question.

Step 2: Untangle the Stimulus

The installation of a new electronic toll system led to fewer delays, shorter travel times, and less pollution per trip. Nonetheless, overall pollution from cars stayed the same.

Step 3: Make a Prediction

The correct answer will answer the central mystery: why is pollution not going down overall? The key here is to notice the discrepancy between the two facts. The benefits described (shorter travel time, tailpipe pollution) are said to be "per car trip." That would be great if the number of car trips stayed constant. However, if more trips were taken, that would solve the mystery. More trips could increase pollution enough to balance out the per-trip reduction.

Step 4: Evaluate the Answer Choices

(C) matches the prediction. If more vehicles use the highway, then reducing pollution per trip might not be enough to make up for the additional cars on the road.

(A) is irrelevant. The price of tolls has no bearing on pollution levels.

(B) is irrelevant. It was never said that the system *eliminated* delays, just that they declined significantly. Even with some delays, there was still a reduction in per-trip pollution, so this doesn't explain why there's still more pollution overall.

(D) does not help. It was never said that *all* trips were shorter, just that they were 10% shorter *on average*. Even if the shortest trips were relatively unchanged, there's still no explanation why pollution didn't drop.

(E) is irrelevant. Even if some people didn't take advantage of the new system, enough must have to result in fewer delays and shorter trips. In that case, pollution still should have dropped, so there's no resolution.

2. (E) Flaw

Step 1: Identify the Question Type

The question asks why the argument presented is *flawed*, clearly indicating a Flaw question.

Step 2: Untangle the Stimulus

The author concludes that not trusting one's neighbors makes one disrespect the law. The evidence is a study that claims neighborhoods where people lock their doors experience more burglaries than other neighborhoods.

Step 3: Make a Prediction

The phrase "leads to" in the conclusion indicates a causal argument. The author is assuming that people locking their doors (implying they don't trust their neighbors) is the reason why there are more burglaries (implying disrespect for the law). Consider the three classic flaws in a causal argument: 1) The author overlooks an alternative cause, i.e., another reason for the higher rate of burglaries. 2) The author might have the causality backward, i.e., maybe people are locking their doors *because* of the burglary rate, not the other way around. 3) It might just be a coincidence. The correct answer will address one of these three common flaws.

Step 4: Evaluate the Answer Choices

(E) is correct, indicating that the author may have the causality backward. Locked doors could be an effect of high burglary rates, not the cause.

(A) is a commonly tested flaw, but not one that's present here. The evidence does not cite anything as sufficient for a particular result. It only cites statistics indicating a correlation.

(B) mentions a "moral conclusion," but the author does not mention morality.

(C) claims the evidence is contradictory, but that's not true. There are different results in different areas, but there's no contradiction.

(D) implies circular reasoning, but the evidence and the conclusion are distinct. The conclusion is about trust and respect for the law, and the evidence is about locking doors and burglaries.

3. (D) Paradox

Step 1: Identify the Question Type

The correct answer will "resolve the apparent discrepancy," making this a Paradox question.

Step 2: Untangle the Stimulus

According to the author, the government is getting more successful at eliminating counterfeit bills. *Yet* counterfeiters are still easily passing off fake bills to merchants and banks.

Step 3: Make a Prediction

The correct answer will address the central mystery: How are counterfeiters getting away with fake bills so easily if the government is cracking down? It helps to notice a key scope shift between the two claims. The *government* is getting better at removing the fake bills from circulation, but counterfeiters are more easily fooling *merchants and banks*. This could be resolved by showing a clear difference between the government and merchants/banks that makes the latter group more susceptible to counterfeiting.

Step 4: Evaluate the Answer Choices

(D) resolves the situation. If merchants and bank tellers are getting lax, they're less likely to spot counterfeit bills. Thus, counterfeiters can get away with more before the government finds the fake bills and takes them away.

(A) is a 180. If such campaigns are more effective than ever, then it's even more of a mystery why the counterfeiters are having an easier time passing along fake bills.

(B) is a 180. If the bills are getting harder to copy, then it's even more of a mystery why counterfeiters are not having difficulty.

(C) is irrelevant. Even if the counterfeiters are unaware of the government's success, that doesn't explain why merchants and banks are being easily fooled while the government is succeeding.

(E) is irrelevant. Even if the government keeps putting more money and effort into removing counterfeit bills from circulation, that still wouldn't affect whether counterfeiters are able to more easily put the fake bills into circulation via merchants and banks. The government is only spending money on pulling the counterfeit bills out, not keeping it from getting put into circulation to begin with.

4. (D) Assumption (Necessary)

Step 1: Identify the Question Type

The question directly asks for an assumption, and one that is "required by the argument," making this a Necessary Assumption question.

Step 2: Untangle the Stimulus

The author concludes (*thus*) that we won't find advanced civilizations within 50 light-years of earth. The evidence is that such a civilization would have discovered us by now and could easily have made contact.

Step 3: Make a Prediction

Sure, if extraterrestrial beings were that close and as technically advanced as us, they *could* have easily contacted us. That doesn't mean they *would* have. Perhaps the evidence they've found suggests that contacting us would be a bad idea. The author just assumes anyone who *could* contact us easily *would*.

Step 4: Evaluate the Answer Choices

(D) must be assumed. After all, using the Denial Test, if other civilizations *didn't* want to contact us, then the author's point is invalid. Life could be out there, they're just ignoring our calls. The author must assume they *would* want to contact us.

(A) is not necessary. It doesn't matter whether scientists are looking specifically for advanced life forms or just for any life forms at all. The argument is about whether scientists will *find* advanced life forms.

(B) is irrelevant. The author's argument is about finding advanced civilizations *within* 50 miles. Whether or not such civilizations exist farther away has no bearing on that argument.

(C) is irrelevant. The argument is not about communicating with and understanding other civilizations. It's only about whether we'll find them or not. Fully deciphering the messages is optional, at best.

(E) is Extreme. It's not important that intelligent life recognize *all* signs of intelligent life on Earth, just that they find anything at all and try to make contact.

5. (B) Paradox

Step 1: Identify the Question Type

The correct answer will "resolve the apparent conflict," making this a Paradox question.

Step 2: Untangle the Stimulus

It was expected that removing traffic lights and street markings on a busy street would lead to more accidents. On the contrary, the number of accidents *decreased*.

Step 3: Make a Prediction

The central mystery is this: why were there fewer accidents when the traffic lights and street markings were taken away? This could be solved by showing some other significant difference that would have resulted in safer driving.

Step 4: Evaluate the Answer Choices

(B) offers a resolution. People started driving more carefully. That's why there were fewer accidents.

(A) is a 180. If people ignored traffic lights and street markings in the first place, then taking those signals away should have done nothing—yet the number of accidents still went down.

(C) is a 180. If people didn't notice, that suggests they were just driving as usual. With no other change in circumstance, it's even harder to understand why the number of accidents went down.

(D) is irrelevant. The mystery revolves around the number of accidents, so safety is the only issue at hand. Besides, this just further suggests that the situation should have been far worse.

(E) does not help. Even if people knew the change was coming, this offers no understanding of what changed to reduce the number of accidents. The mystery remains.

6. (B) Flaw

Step 1: Identify the Question Type

The correct answer will describe why the argument is "vulnerable to criticism," a common phrase that indicates a Flaw question.

Step 2: Untangle the Stimulus

The argument being made is that body size universally influences mating decisions. The evidence comes from studies of college students and personal ads.

Step 3: Make a Prediction

The author is drawing a conclusion about "all societies" in general based on a very particular subset of people: college students and people using personal ads. This is a classic case of representativeness: basing a very broad conclusion on a potentially unrepresentative sample. The correct answer will identify this illogical argumentative technique.

Step 4: Evaluate the Answer Choices

(B) accurately identifies the likelihood of an unrepresentative sample in the evidence.

(A) is a Distortion. The author is not claiming one thing causes another. If it's interpreted that way, it could be suggested that body size is the cause of mating decisions. However, in that case, it makes no sense to raise the possibility of a third event that could cause both body size and mating decisions.

(C) is a Distortion. The author is not making any claim about cause and effect. And even if one interprets the conclusion to suggest that body size causes mating decisions, there's no stated evidence about mating decisions having multiple causes.

(D) reverses and distorts the logic of the argument. The author uses a claim about certain people to draw a conclusion about entire societies, not the other way around. Further, the author does not apply anything to anyone individually.

(E) is a Distortion. This suggests a different representative issue: small sample size. However, there's no evidence of the sample size. The author could have looked over a very large number of reports and analyses. The representative flaw here is based on the *type* of people involved in the evidence, not the *number*.

7. (A) Assumption (Necessary)

Step 1: Identify the Question Type

The question directly asks for an assumption, and one that is *required*, making this a Necessary Assumption question.

Step 2: Untangle the Stimulus

The journalist concludes that the new mayor is not introspective. The evidence is that the mayor is bold and makes confident, certain assertions.

Step 3: Make a Prediction

The evidence is solely about the mayor's boldness and assertiveness, but the conclusion is about being introspective. These are completely different concepts. The journalist assumes they are connected. Specifically, the journalist assumes that being bold and assertive prevents one from being introspective.

Step 4: Evaluate the Answer Choices

(A) connects the mismatched concepts and is correct.

(B) confirms that assertiveness makes the mayor popular, but it does nothing to justify a conclusion about being introspective.

(C) connects boldness and assertiveness, but the conclusion about being introspective remains disconnected and unsupported.

(D) is a Distortion. Even if people who lack confidence are introspective, that doesn't mean bold and assertive people can't be.

(E) is irrelevant. The new mayor *is* bold, so it doesn't matter what people who *aren't* bold are like. Besides, this still fails to connect the conclusion's mismatched concept of being introspective.

8. (E) Inference

Step 1: Identify the Question Type

The question stem indicates that the stimulus will be a series of statements (instead of a full argument), and they will provide support for the correct answer. That means the correct answer will be an inference backed up by the stimulus.

Step 2: Untangle the Stimulus

In a study, macaque monkeys less than a week old imitated some, but not all, gestures made by scientists. The ones they *did* imitate (lip smacking and sticking out the tongue) are ones adult macaques use with babies. The other gestures are not used this way.

Step 3: Make a Prediction

Based on the results, this suggests that baby macaques must innately know which gestures would be used by adult macaques and will only imitate those particular gestures.

Step 4: Evaluate the Answer Choices

(E) is supported, as gestures used by adult macaques are the only gestures the babies imitated.

(A) is a 180. If they naturally mimicked "whatever they see," then they would have also imitated the open/closed mouth and hand gestures. So, this statement must be false based on the stimulus.

(B) is not supported. It is only stated that they *don't* imitate hand gestures, not that they *can't*.

(C) is not supported. While these gestures are used "when interacting with babies," there's no suggestion that they are for entertainment purposes. The gestures might be used as a form of communication.

(D) is not supported. The babies might be mimicking the gestures, but that does not suggest that they think the human scientists are actually monkeys. The babies might simply recognize the gestures regardless of who or what species uses them.

9. (B) Main Point

Step 1: Identify the Question Type

The correct answer will express the "conclusion drawn in the argument" making this a Main Point question.

Step 2: Untangle the Stimulus

The author presents the view of "some scientists": the skeletons are of people with a growth disorder. As usually happens when an argument opens with *some people's* view, the author disagrees: the skeletons were of a unique species of people who just got smaller over time. The author then presents evidence that contradicts the "growth disorder" view and supports the "smaller people" view.

Step 3: Make a Prediction

The main point is the author's rejection of the scientists' view: the skeletons were of particular people who became smaller over time, not people with a growth disorder.

Step 4: Evaluate the Answer Choices

(B) is correct, accurately expressing the author's point of view.

(A) presents the scientists' view, but completely misses the author's rejection of that view in favor of an alternate one.

(C) is merely evidence that contradicts the scientists' view. It is not the author's conclusion.

(D) is merely evidence in support of the conclusion drawn by the author.

(E) may be assumed by the author, but it is not the conclusion stated regarding the skeletons found in Indonesia.

10. (C) Strengthen

Step 1: Identify the Question Type

The question directly asks for something that will strengthen the argument.

Step 2: Untangle the Stimulus

The author concludes ([*t*]*herefore*) that the atmosphere would get cooler when there's more snow and ice on Earth's surface. The evidence is that snow and ice reflect more sunlight to space than water and land, and the atmosphere gets cooler as more sunlight is reflected.

Step 3: Make a Prediction

The evidence is only half helpful. It adequately shows the cooling effect that snow- and ice-covered land has on the atmosphere. However, the evidence does not describe the effect of water and land on the atmosphere. While they may not reflect as much sunlight, they could possibly have a *greater* cooling effect in other ways. The author assumes otherwise: that snow and ice will have a greater cooling effect than land and water. The correct answer will verify this.

Step 4: Evaluate the Answer Choices

(C) is correct. If water and land have the effect of warming the atmosphere and snow and ice have a cooling effect, that strengthens the suggestion that covering more land with snow and ice will lead to more cooling.

(A) is irrelevant. It doesn't matter how cold it has to be to snow in the first place. The argument is about whether having snow on the ground will make the atmosphere even colder.

(B) is a 180. If there are other factors to consider, then it's possible that the reflection of sunlight by snow and ice will not be enough to cool the atmosphere.

(D) is a 180. If heat comes from sunlight passing through the atmosphere, and ice and snow reflect *more* sunlight through the atmosphere, that would contradict the idea that more sunlight would make the atmosphere cooler.

(E) is an Irrelevant Comparison. The argument is about ice and snow versus water and land, not different colors of land/soil.

11. (C) Point at Issue

Step 1: Identify the Question Type

The correct answer will identify a claim that two speakers "disagree over," making this a Point at Issue question.

Step 2: Untangle the Stimulus

Nick is arguing that the university should not hire the Pincus family's competitor to build the library because the Pincus family has donated to the university, and universities should be loyal to donors. Pedro argues that there should be no preferential treatment to donors and that the decision should be based solely on which bid is most competitive.

Step 3: Make a Prediction

Pedro and Nick disagree about the criteria for choosing a bid. Pedro only considers the competitiveness, while Nick says to consider donor loyalty. This stems from a more basic issue:

Nick feels donor loyalty should influence the decision, while Pedro says donors shouldn't receive any special privileges. The correct answer will address the issue of whether donor loyalty should have any influence.

Step 4: Evaluate the Answer Choices

(C) is correct. Nick feels that donations do confer privileges, as he argues that the Pincus family should get preferential treatment because of their donations. Pedro directly argues otherwise: donors should not get any special privileges.

(A) is a Distortion. Nick definitely agrees with **(A)**. Pedro might also agree that loyalty can be considered for *some* business decisions. It just doesn't apply here because there *is* no loyalty. Donations (according to Pedro) don't confer such standing.

(B) is not supported. Neither Nick nor Pedro make any suggestion about the Pincus family's motivation. It's actually possible that Nick and Pedro agree that the Pincus family had self-serving motivations, but Pedro simply argues that they don't deserve any special privileges.

(D) is not supported. Neither Nick nor Pedro make any distinction between new and long-term donors.

(E) is not supported. Neither Nick nor Pedro indicate which bid is more competitive. That cannot be determined with certainty from either speaker.

12. (A) Strengthen

Step 1: Identify the Question Type

The correct answer will "strongly support" the conclusion, making this a Strengthen question. While most fill-in-the-blank questions are Inference questions, this one is different because the blank is preceded by the Keyword *since*. That indicates that the blank will be an additional piece of evidence in support of the author's conclusion. The question could also conceivably be categorized as an Assumption question because whatever fills in the blank will need to tie together the evidence and conclusion.

Step 2: Untangle the Stimulus

Because new antibiotics such as ampicillin are more profitable than older ones like penicillin, drug companies want to stop producing old antibiotics and start pushing the new ones. However, the author concludes ([*t*]*hus*) that these new antibiotics are likely to lead to an outbreak of diseases caused by drug-resistant bacteria. The stated evidence is that these new antibiotics kill a wider variety of bacteria than do older ones.

Step 3: Make a Prediction

The evidence is solely about how many bacteria are killed. From that, the author makes a drastic jump to the conclusion, warning about a potential outbreak. The author must assume that killing off a wide variety of bacteria will somehow lead to an outbreak of drug-resistant-bacteria-borne diseases. The correct answer will verify this assumption.

Step 4: Evaluate the Answer Choices

(A) is correct, connecting the killing of many bacteria to the flourishing of drug-resistant bacteria—the supposed cause of the predicted outbreak.

(B) is irrelevant. The prior use of older antibiotics has no effect on determining whether the new ones will lead to an outbreak.

(C) is irrelevant and a 180 at worst. The price and profit margin of penicillin has no bearing on whether the new antibiotics would lead to an outbreak. At worst, if the profit margin of penicillin *does* increase, drug companies may not stop making it. So, the new antibiotics might not be pushed as much, and the predicted outbreak could potentially be avoided.

(D) is irrelevant and a 180 at worst. The cost of treatment has no bearing on whether an outbreak will occur. If anything, a higher cost might lead fewer people to use the new antibiotics, thus *reducing* the possibility of an outbreak.

(E) is a 180. This suggests that ampicillin (one of the new antibiotics) can kill off a lot of bacteria that are currently drug-resistant, making it *less* likely that such drug-resistant bacteria will cause an outbreak.

13. (E) Flaw

Step 1: Identify the Question Type

The correct answer will describe why the reasoning is *flawed*, making this a Flaw question.

Step 2: Untangle the Stimulus

Weingarten argues that zoos place animals in unnatural environments in order to amuse humans, thus making zoos unethical. *However*, the author concludes that Weingarten's claim should be rejected, i.e., zoos are not unethical. The evidence is that Weingarten is okay with people having pets, which also involves placing animals in unnatural environments to amuse humans.

Step 3: Make a Prediction

There is some logic in calling out Weingarten's hypocrisy. He has two conflicting views: zoos are unethical, but pets are okay. One of them must be mistaken, but which one? The author just decides the claim about zoos is mistaken. However, it's possible that Weingarten is *correct* about that claim, but is mistaken in his approval of owning pets. So, the author's flaw is rejecting a claim solely because of a contradiction, when that claim could just as likely be accepted in favor of the competing claim.

Step 4: Evaluate the Answer Choices

(E) is correct. The author rejects Weingarten's claim merely because of Weingarten's inconsistent view regarding pets.

(A) is a Distortion. The author's argument is based on Weingarten's view that owning pets is okay. There's no implication or assumption that Weingarten himself actually owns any.

(B) is inaccurate. The author is comparing the general idea of zoos to the general idea of owning pets. No particular cases are mentioned.

(C) is inaccurate. Weingarten's conclusion is clear: zoos are unethical. There's no misrepresentation.

(D) invokes the flaw of necessity vs. sufficiency. However, there are no conditional statements, and nothing is deemed necessary to claiming a practice is unethical.

14. (E) Principle (Identify/Strengthen)

Step 1: Identify the Question Type

The correct answer will be a principle that will *justify* an argument. That makes this an Identify the Principle question that acts like a Strengthen question. Take note that there are two speakers, and the question asks for the principle that justifies the *first* speaker's claims.

Step 2: Untangle the Stimulus

The activist argues that President Zagel should resign because people feel she rigged the election, making her ineffective. President Zagel argues that she can't resign. Her evidence is that two other presidents resigned in the past 10 years, and her resigning would cause the world to view her country as politically unstable.

Step 3: Make a Prediction

With any recommendation, the assumption is that the support provided is enough to outweigh any considerations against that recommendation. In this case, the activist's support for recommending the president's resignation is her inability to govern effectively. The president provides another consideration: the world may perceive her country as politically unstable. So, the activist is assuming that the president's ineffectiveness outweighs the potential of a bad reputation for the country. The correct answer will be a general rule that validates that assumption.

Step 4: Evaluate the Answer Choices

(E) matches the prediction. If effective leadership is more important than a good reputation, then the activist has a stronger case than the president.

(A) is a Distortion. The activist's argument is not about making the country politically stable or fixing the election system. The activist is only concerned about removing the president for the sake of effective governing.

(B) is a Faulty Use of Detail. Only the president seems to be concerned about the country's reputation. That activist is only concerned about effective governing.

(C) is an Irrelevant Comparison. There's no indication whether previous scandals were any more or less serious than the president's rigging scandal, so this offers no basis for making a judgment call about the president.

(D) is Out of Scope. There is no conclusive evidence, so, while the activist may agree with this claim, it offers no justification for ousting a president based merely on a "widespread belief."

15. (A) Flaw

Step 1: Identify the Question Type

The correct answer will describe an "error of reasoning," making this a Flaw question.

Step 2: Untangle the Stimulus

A book claims that successful people always benefited from luck.

> *If*   *successful*   →   *luck*

But the author claims this is ridiculous; i.e., luck is not a factor. The evidence is that success requires hard work.

> *If*   *successful*   →   *hard work*

Step 3: Make a Prediction

The first issue that may stand out is the author's implication that hard work and luck are mutually exclusive. In other words, the author is erroneously assuming you can't be lucky *and* work hard at the same time. Unfortunately, none of the answers address that scope shift, so there must be another flaw. In this case, the phrases "without exception" and "requires" indicate some Formal Logic. In essence, the book claims success requires luck (as all successful people benefited from luck). The author argues that success requires hard work, implying that luck is not *good enough*, i.e., not sufficient. However, the book never claimed luck was sufficient, just that it was necessary. The correct answer will point out the author's mistake in suggesting otherwise.

Step 4: Evaluate the Answer Choices

(A) accurately describes the flaw of necessity vs. sufficiency. The author mistakenly takes the book's claim that luck is required and assumes the book is suggesting that luck is sufficient.

(B) is a Distortion. The view presented by the author (success requires hard work) is not attributed to a particular source. It's said to be known by "anyone who has studied successful people," so there is no need to establish any authority.

(C) suggests circular reasoning, but the evidence and the conclusion are distinct. The premise regarding hard work is not based on any assumptions regarding the conclusion about luck.

(D) is a Distortion. The relationship between causes (luck, hard work) and effects (success) is consistent. The author never gets it backwards (e.g., suggesting that success is the cause of luck).

(E) is a 180. The author *does* attack the substance, questioning the involvement of luck. The author makes no attack on the book itself.

16. (B) Principle (Parallel)

Step 1: Identify the Question Type

The correct answer will be a specific circumstance that "conforms most closely to [a] principle," making this a Principle question. The principle will be applied to the answer choices, but the principle is not given. It is *illustrated* by the specific argument provided. Thus, the principle must be identified first, and then reapplied to the answers. This is a rare Parallel Principle question.

Step 2: Untangle the Stimulus

The president concludes that it's a good thing the media raised a discussion of the university's standards. Even though the media was mistaken, the president states that it's important to stay vigilant regarding academic standards.

Step 3: Make a Prediction

To formulate the principle, take the president's specific argument and broaden the scope. In this case, the principle is that it's good to discuss a certain topic because, even if there was a mistaken accusation regarding that topic, it's important to pay attention to that topic. The correct answer will apply the exact logic of that principle to another specific situation.

Step 4: Evaluate the Answer Choices

(B) applies the principle perfectly. It's good to discuss a certain topic (oversight) because, even though there was a mistaken accusation regarding that topic (the scandal was mistakenly attributed to oversight, but was really a single case of corruption), it's important to pay attention to that first topic (oversight).

(A) does not match. There is no mistaken accusation. Plus, it's indicating a causal nature between the two topics, and praising the discussion of both of them, which doesn't align with the original argument.

(C) does not match. In the original argument, there was concern that it was one thing (low academic standards), when it was really another thing (one case of dishonesty). In (C), it is *both* things (lack of oversight and corruption). Furthermore,

it is not clear that the *harm* mentioned is parallel to the results of the case of dishonesty in the original argument.

(D) does not match. This condemns the mistaken accusation, which completely contradicts the more positive "it's okay because at least we're talking about something important" tone of the original argument.

(E) does not match. This argument praises the discussion of corruption not because of the importance of staying vigilant, but because corruption played "the largest role in the scandal." The original argument did not weigh the role of standards against anything else.

17. (C) Strengthen/Weaken (Evaluate the Argument)

Step 1: Identify the Question Type

The question asks for something "useful to know in evaluating" the argument. That makes this a variation of a Strengthen/Weaken question known as Evaluate the Argument. The correct answer will raise a question that, depending on how it's answered, would affect the validity of the argument. In essence, it will pose a question about the argument's assumption.

Step 2: Untangle the Stimulus

The politician is arguing that replacing the city's street signs with new, more readable signs is waste of time and money. The evidence is that nobody's complaining about the current signs.

Step 3: Make a Prediction

The politician makes two assumptions. First, the politician assumes that public opinion is the primary deciding factor. Even though the public hasn't complained, there could still be good reason to replace the signs. Second, the politician claims that the project would be a waste of time and money. That is only true if the time and money would be otherwise spent on something better or more useful. The correct answer will question either one of those assumptions.

Step 4: Evaluate the Answer Choices

(C) is correct, questioning the assumption about what the time and money would be otherwise spent on. The plan is to replace the signs "over the next decade." If the city already replaces at least 10% of its signs every year, then the plan is not a waste of time—all signs would have been replaced anyway. However, if the city only replaced a very small percentage of its signs annually (e.g., 1%), then the politician's point is valid: why spend all that money replacing signs that people are okay with?

(A) is irrelevant. Regardless of what specific features are used, there's no way of evaluating whether installing the new signs would be worthwhile or not.

(B) is an Irrelevant Comparison. Regardless of which signs are more expensive, the politician's argument is unaffected. Replacing the current signs could waste money no matter how much the new signs cost, whether they're cheaper or more expensive.

(D) is also an Irrelevant Comparison. Other cities may have different reasons to either replace (e.g., people there *do* complain) or not replace (e.g., not enough money). Their decisions offer no legitimate basis for judging the politician's decision.

(E) is irrelevant. It doesn't matter how the new signs were designed or who was consulted. It's still uncertain if installing those signs would be worthwhile or not.

18. (A) Assumption (Necessary)

Step 1: Identify the Question Type

The question asks for something the argument "requires assuming," making this a Necessary Assumption question.

Step 2: Untangle the Stimulus

The author concludes ([*t*]*herefore*) that most of the surveyed scientists reject the Minsk Hypothesis. The evidence is that the Minsk Hypothesis is contradicted by combining Wang's Law with the results of the Brown-Eisler Experiment, two things accepted or recognized by almost all scientists surveyed.

Step 3: Make a Prediction

The author claims that the scientists know about and accept two separate pieces of evidence (Wang's Law, Brown-Eisler Experiment). However, the Minsk Hypothesis is contradicted by *combining* those two pieces of evidence. The author has spotted that issue, but there's no evidence that the scientists have made the connection yet. It's only stated that they know about the two pieces separately. The author must assume that the scientists have already made the connection tying Wang's Law and the Brown-Eisler Experiment to the Minsk Hypothesis.

Step 4: Evaluate the Answer Choices

(A) is correct, as it must be assumed. Using the Denial Test, if the scientists were *not* aware of the connection to the Minsk Hypothesis, they would have no basis for rejecting it. The author must assume they are aware of the connection.

(B) is Extreme. These do not have to be the *exact* same group of scientists. It's possible there are one or two scientists who accept Wang's Law but haven't heard about the Brown-Eisler Experiment yet (or vice versa). Such anomalies would not affect the author's conclusion.

(C) is irrelevant. All that matters is that the scientists know the results. It makes no difference whether or not they know *how* those results were obtained.

(D) is irrelevant. The conclusion is about the "scientists surveyed," not about scientists in general.

(E) is irrelevant. Even if Wang's Law has not been entirely confirmed, the scientists still accept it. Proving Wang's Law true is not necessary.

19. (D) Principle (Identify/Strengthen)

Step 1: Identify the Question Type

The correct answer will be a principle that "helps to justify" the argument, making this an Identify the Principle question that acts like a Strengthen question.

Step 2: Untangle the Stimulus

The author concludes ([*t*]*hus*) that even the most skillful translation of a book will be flawed. The evidence is that a translation cannot stay entirely faithful to both the meaning of the original text and the original author's style. Some compromise must be made.

Step 3: Make a Prediction

The author assumes that the compromise made automatically results in a "flawed approximation." The correct answer will be a general rule that validates that assumption.

Step 4: Evaluate the Answer Choices

(D) is correct, confirming the author's assumption that the compromise between meaning and style automatically results in a flawed approximation.

(A) is a Distortion. The author never argues that the meaning or the style *should* be compromised, just that something inevitably *is*. Besides, this offers no justification for the characterization of translations as "flawed approximations."

(B) raises the question of whether a compromise is successful, a concept about which the author makes no claim.

(C) is irrelevant. The balance between faithfulness to meaning and faithfulness to style does nothing to justify calling any translations a "flawed approximation."

(E) is a Faulty Use of Detail. It is consistent with the opening claim that any translation (even the most skillful) cannot be faithful to both meaning and style. However, it does nothing to justify the conclusion that such translations are "flawed approximations."

20. (D) Inference (EXCEPT)

Step 1: Identify the Question Type

The correct answer will be based on accepting all the given statements as true. That makes this an Inference question. However, while most Inference questions ask for something supported or true, this question does not. Here, four answers "could be true," while the correct answer will be the exception: the one that cannot be true (i.e., it must be false).

Step 2: Untangle the Stimulus

According to the sociologists, certain technologies (TV, phones, electronic media) lead to uncritical thinking. Unfortunately, critical thinking is the *only* way to protect against demagogues that exploit people's emotions to distort reality.

If	adequately protected against demagogues	→	critical thinking
If	~ critical thinking	→	~ adequately protected against demagogues

Step 3: Make a Prediction

With an Inference question asking for such an absolute answer (the one that *must* be false), look for the strongest claims that can be more directly contradicted. In this case, the sociologist claims that critical thinking is the *only* adequate protection against demagogues. Any answer that suggests something else is adequate or critical reasoning is not enough will absolutely contradict the sociologist, and thus could not be true.

Step 4: Evaluate the Answer Choices

(D) is correct. According to the sociologist, critical thinking is the *only* adequate protection. In that case, it *cannot* be true that an orderly system of government by itself would be adequate.

(A) could be true. Technology does encourage uncritical thinking, which would make people susceptible to demagogues. However, there's no way to know for sure whether demagogues are present or not in any given society. It's possible (even if unlikely) that demagogues only appear in non-technological societies, making the technological ones fortunate in that there are no demagogues to exploit their uncritical thinking.

(B) could be true. Demagogues exploit people's emotions, but it's never said that they're the only type of people to do so. There certainly could be other people who exploit emotions.

(C) is an Irrelevant Comparison that could be true. The sociologist makes no comparison between highly emotional people and less emotional people, so it's very possible highly emotional people are more easily exploited.

(E) could be true. The sociologist offers no information about the erosion of media freedoms, so this claim could be true or false. There's no support either way.

21. (E) Weaken

Step 1: Identify the Question Type

The question directly asks for something that weakens the given argument.

Step 2: Untangle the Stimulus

The author concludes ([*t*]*hus*) that taking lots of B vitamins and folic acid can reduce the risk of getting Alzheimer's disease. The evidence is that B vitamins and folic acid convert homocysteine, a substance found in high levels in people with Alzheimer's, into other substances that are not connected to Alzheimer's.

Step 3: Make a Prediction

Most directly, the author is assuming that removing homocysteine will certainly reduce people's risk of Alzheimer's, as if there were no other way the risk could stay constant. This could be weakened by showing that the risk *doesn't* change or that removing homocysteine would have no effect.

However, there's also an implication of causality. Homocysteine levels are higher in people with Alzheimer's, but the author is implying that homocysteine is the *cause* of Alzheimer's, so reducing homocysteine would remove a potential cause. There are three ways to weaken this causal argument: 1) Show an alternative cause of Alzheimer's. 2) Show the author mistakenly reversed causality; i.e., having Alzheimer's is the cause of high homocysteine levels, not the other way around. 3) Indicate that it's just a coincidence and that the two factors are in fact unconnected.

Step 4: Evaluate the Answer Choices

(E) weakens the argument by indicating that the author may have the causality reversed. If the high levels of homocysteine are caused *by* Alzheimer's, then replacing homocysteine would have no effect. Something else is causing Alzheimer's, and the B vitamins and folic acid wouldn't stop that from happening.

(A) has no effect on the argument. Even if lots of Alzheimer's patients have normal homocysteine levels, high levels could still create a greater risk of developing the disease. In that case, taking B vitamins and folic acid won't guarantee anything, but it could still reduce the risk.

(B) is Out of Scope. The author's argument is about reducing the risk of Alzheimer's. Even if there are other harmful effects, the risk of Alzheimer's would still be reduced.

(C) is also Out of Scope. This would be a problem if the author only recommended supplements. However, even if supplements are inefficient, there could be other ways to increase B vitamins and folic acid without compromising efficiency. Thus, the author's argument goes unaffected.

(D) is also Out of Scope. Even if there are other factors that affect the risk of Alzheimer's, it's still possible that replacing homocysteine could have *some* effect of its own and reduce the risk.

22. (E) Role of a Statement

Step 1: Identify the Question Type

The question presents a claim from the stimulus and asks for "the role played" by that claim in the argument. That makes this a Role of a Statement question.

Step 2: Untangle the Stimulus

The advocate concludes ("[a]s a result") that increasing a good's price will benefit people with the most money, not the people who actually need that good. This contradicts the economists, who argue that price gouging (increasing price in absence of competition) favors those who need that good because they're the ones willing to pay for it. *But* the advocate claims that "willingness to pay" and *need* do not correlate with one another.

Step 3: Make a Prediction

The claim in question (which follows the Keyword [*b*]*ut*) is the advocate's rebuttal of the economist's view. That rebuttal is then used to support the advocate's conclusion in the final sentence. The correct answer will address the claim's role as a rebuttal or as support for the advocate's conclusion, or both.

Step 4: Evaluate the Answer Choices

(E) matches the claim's purpose, albeit in a convoluted way. The "reasoning that [the argument] rejects" is the economist's view. That view (price gouging reduces buyers to those who need the good) assumes that the more someone is willing to pay for a good, the more that person *needs* that good. The claim in question denies that assumption, just as this answer indicates.

(A) is a Distortion. The advocate is disputing a purported *effect* of an action (price gouging benefiting those who need a certain good) and claiming a different *effect* will occur (price gouging will benefit those with the most money). The advocate neither disputes nor advocates for any *explanations*.

(B) is incorrect. The conclusion is the last sentence, not the claim in question.

(C) is a 180. The claim is not part of the reasoning being disputed; it's the evidence *against* the reasoning being disputed.

(D) is a 180. The advocate does not question the validity of the claim in question. The advocate accepts that claim and uses it to reject the economist's view.

23. (D) Strengthen

Step 1: Identify the Question Type

The question directly asks for an answer that will strengthen the argument.

Step 2: Untangle the Stimulus

The zoologist concludes ([*t*]*hus*) that prehistoric cave bears were not exclusively herbivores (plant-eaters). The evidence is that blood samples from modern meat-eating bears had the same level of heavy nitrogen as bone samples from prehistoric cave bears, and meat-eaters usually have more heavy nitrogen in their tissues than herbivores.

Step 3: Make a Prediction

If both prehistoric cave bears and modern bears had the same concentration of heavy nitrogen, it would certainly suggest a similar diet. So, if the modern bear eats meat, it stands to reason that the prehistoric bears did, too. The problem is that the zoologist compared blood samples to bone samples. That assumes that heavy nitrogen levels are consistent from blood to bone. If bone samples usually have a higher concentration of heavy nitrogen than blood, then the prehistoric bears would have had lower levels in their blood, which would suggest a different (perhaps all-plant) diet. To strengthen the zoologist's claim, it should be shown that heavy nitrogen levels do not vary between bone and blood.

Step 4: Evaluate the Answer Choices

(D) strengthens the argument. This confirms that heavy nitrogen levels stay constant between bone and blood, making the comparison between prehistoric bones and modern blood more valid.

(A) is Out of Scope. It doesn't matter where the heavy nitrogen comes from. The argument only depends on the amount of heavy nitrogen found in the bears.

(B) is Out of Scope. What's important is that the ultimate level of heavy nitrogen in blood can be inferred from bone samples. The *rate* of accumulation is irrelevant.

(C) is also Out of Scope. The number of samples doesn't matter. All that matters are the results.

(E) is an Irrelevant Comparison. What matters is that the levels of the prehistoric bears match *any* bear that eats any amount of meat from any source. Differing heavy nitrogen levels among differing types of bears or bears with meat from different sources, does nothing to support the zoologist's conclusion about prehistoric bears.

24. (B) Assumption (Necessary)

Step 1: Identify the Question Type

The correct answer will be an "assumption required" by the argument, making this a Necessary Assumption question.

Step 2: Untangle the Stimulus

The phrase "[t]hey are mistaken" indicates the biologist's conclusion, a rejection of the computer scientists' view. They claim a computer program encapsulating the information in a human genome is all you need to create artificial intelligence. The biologist rejects this claim, thus concluding that human genome information is not enough. The evidence is that the brains are controlled by the "interactions of proteins" within the genome.

Step 3: Make a Prediction

The biologist is implying that the interactions of proteins are what really govern the human brain (and would thus lead to intelligence). If the biologist claims that encapsulating the information in a genome is not enough, the biologist must be assuming that the genome does not provide information on the interactions of proteins.

Step 4: Evaluate the Answer Choices

(B) is correct, making the necessary connection between genome information and the inability to get protein interaction.

(A) is a Distortion. It is not *necessary* that computers are incapable of simulating the protein interactions. It's merely necessary that encapsulating genome information is not enough to provide those interactions. Even if those interactions *could* be simulated by a computer, the biologist could still argue that genome information would not be enough to create those simulations. More would be needed.

(C) is Extreme. Modeling the human brain does not have to be the *only* way. Even if there were other ways, the biologist could still claim that encapsulating genome information would not be enough.

(D) is not necessary. It doesn't have to be difficult to get that information. Even if it were really easy for a computer, the biologist could still have a point that such information would not be enough.

(E) is an Irrelevant Comparison. It doesn't matter which program would be harder to write. The question is whether encapsulating genome information would be enough by itself for making artificial intelligence, regardless of the difficulty of programming protein interactions.

25. (A) Inference

Step 1: Identify the Question Type

The correct answer will be "strongly supported" by the information provided. That makes this an Inference question.

Step 2: Untangle the Stimulus

The stimulus describes an advertising ploy that involves giving away free computers that constantly play ads. The ads adapt to people's Internet usage so that the ads reflect the users' interests. Advertisers can afford this because the ads lead to increased sales.

Step 3: Make a Prediction

It's hard to predict exactly what the correct answer will say, but keep the general tone and message in mind. In this case, advertisers are giving away free computers that play targeted ads, and the plan is working. Watch out for answers that distort the facts, introduce unsupported elements, or are too strong in language.

Step 4: Evaluate the Answer Choices

(A) is supported. If advertisers "can afford to offer the computers for free," the plan must be working to some degree. Thus, it's logical that at least *some* people are buying the advertisers' products who otherwise wouldn't.

(B) is Extreme. This denies any other way to get effective use out of giving away free computers. While the Internet-based system seems to work, there could still be *some* way to use free computers as an advertising ploy without the Internet.

(C) is unsupported. There's no suggestion that people who get these computers spend very little online to begin with. The suggestion is that some people who *do* get these computers just start buying *more*.

(D) is not supported. In order to afford to give away the computers, the advertisers *have* to get increased sales, but they don't necessarily *have* to play adds continuously. They might be just as able to offer such computers even if the ads only popped up every 15–30 minutes.

(E) is not supported. There is no indication that consumers have any ability to prevent information from being sent at any time.

26. (E) Parallel Flaw

Step 1: Identify the Question Type

The correct answer will be reasoning "similar to" that in the stimulus. Furthermore, that reasoning will be *flawed*, making this a Parallel Flaw question.

Step 2: Untangle the Stimulus

According to the author, some eloquent speakers can impress audiences with clear, vivid messages. Because of this, the author concludes that speakers who use obscenity, who are not eloquent, are incapable of impressing audiences.

Step 3: Make a Prediction

The flaw is that the evidence is only about some people who *are* eloquent. The evidence provides no information about ineloquent speakers, and therefore offers no justification that they can't also impress audiences. The correct answer will be flawed in the exact same way. The argument will claim that some people of a certain type (eloquent speakers) can perform a particular action (impress audiences), and then conclude that people who are *not* that type *cannot* perform that action.

Step 4: Evaluate the Answer Choices

(E) matches the flawed logic. It claims that some people of a certain type (sculptors) can perform a particular action (produce significant art), and then concludes that people who are *not* that type *cannot* perform that action. Like the original, there's no justification that musicians cannot produce significant art just like sculptors do.

(A) does not match. The logic here is not flawed. If *any* culture with no myths has no moral certainties, then the culture cited without myths cannot have certainties.

(B) does not match. The reasoning here is certainly illogical, but for various reasons that do not compare to the original. Here, some people of a certain type (authors who write one page a day) can perform a particular action (produce one book a year). However, this argument doesn't claim that serious authors (who don't write one page a day) cannot produce one book a year. And, unlike the original, the conclusion is about people who *can* write a book a year. This argument is just not parallel to the original.

(C) does not match. This compares centers of industry to centers of commerce, and centers of commerce are always centers of industry. They're part of the same group. The original argument compares people in one group (eloquent speakers) to people who are *not* in that group (those who use obscenity). This argument is certainly illogical, but not in the same way.

(D) does not match. The concept of [*m*]*ost* does not align with the original. Further, the conclusion does not outright reject the possibility of certain people being able to perform a certain act. This just claims one person *probably* wouldn't like something. It's not entirely logical, but it's not flawed in the same way as the original.

Section II: Reading Comprehension
Passage 1: Muscle Memory

Q#	Question Type	Correct	Difficulty
1	Global	C	★
2	Logic Reasoning (Method of Arg.)	B	★
3	Inference	A	★
4	Inference	C	★★
5	Global	D	★★★★
6	Inference	D	★★
7	Detail	E	★★★

Passage 2: Eileen Gray

Q#	Question Type	Correct	Difficulty
8	Global	B	★
9	Inference	E	★★★
10	Inference	E	★★
11	Detail	C	★★★
12	Inference	A	★★★
13	Logic Reasoning (Principle)	B	★★★
14	Inference	C	★★★★

Passage 3: Mesolithic Woodland Clearings

Q#	Question Type	Correct	Difficulty
15	Global	B	★★
16	Detail	B	★★
17	Logic Reasoning (Strengthen)	E	★★★
18	Inference	D	★★
19	Logic Function	D	★
20	Inference	A	★★
21	Inference	A	★★★
22	Logic Reasoning (Parallel Reasoning)	E	★★★★

Passage 4: Specific Performance

Q#	Question Type	Correct	Difficulty
23	Logic Reasoning (Principle)	B	★★
24	Inference	C	★★★
25	Global	E	★★
26	Inference	A	★★
27	Logic Reasoning (Strengthen)	C	★★★

Passage 1: Muscle Memory

Step 1: Read the Passage Strategically

Sample Roadmap

line #	Keyword/phrase	¶ Margin notes
Passage A		
1	puzzling	Muscle memory common
3	yet	
6	seems easier	
7	even if	but unexplained
9	must	
10	One potential explanation	Auth theory:
17	But	more exercise → more neurons → more muscle fibers
26	Although	
29	also possible	Theory 2: It's mental
30	nothing; :	
Passage B		
39–40	think they know why	Scientists: muscles retain something
42	Because	Muscles need nuclei for protein
44	Previous	More exercise → more nuclei
49	had thought	Prev idea: extra nuclei die
52	recent	New study w/ mice: muscles got more nuclei
57	but	
58	Since	Nuclei don't die = cellular muscle memory

Discussion

Passage A gets right to the **Topic**: Muscle memory—a phenomenon in which bodybuilders who stop training are able to gain muscles more easily when they start working out again. The author expresses surprise that no explanation exists for this. Finding an explanation is the **Scope** of the passage.

The author then presents two theories. First, in the second paragraph, the author suggests neurons play a role. When weightlifting, neurons stimulate muscle fibers. More weightlifting leads to more neurons, which leads to more muscle fibers being stimulated. The body then adapts so it can continue stimulating that increased number of muscle fibers. When one quits and comes back to weightlifting, the body adapts to start where the weightlifter left off.

In the third paragraph, the author offers a different theory: it could just be in your head. When you stop training and then come back, you simply remember what your body could handle in the past. So, you don't start off slowly any more, and you get back to building muscles more quickly. The author never provides any support for the theories, so the **Purpose** is merely to present the two theories. The **Main Idea** is that muscle memory may involve neurons and muscle fibers, or it may be mental, but there's no definitive explanation.

Muscle memory is also the **Topic** of passage B. However, unlike the previous author, the author of passage B claims in the first paragraph that scientists *have* come up with an explanation. This explanation serves as the **Scope** of passage B, and the **Purpose** is to inform the reader of that explanation.

Paragraph 2 starts off with the science of muscle-building. Muscle-building requires proteins, and muscle cells have multiple nuclei to make those proteins. When exercising, muscle cells grow and merge with other cells to absorb even more nuclei. However, when exercising stops, researchers assume that the extra nuclei just die off.

Paragraph 3 introduces a study of mice that suggests otherwise. In that study, the muscle cells in mice grew and, as expected, gained new nuclei. However, when they stopped exercising, the nuclei did *not* die. They stuck around so that, should the mice start exercising again, the muscle cells still have the extra nuclei to start making the extra proteins. That leads to the **Main Idea**: new studies suggest that it's easier for people who had exercised before to build muscles because muscle cells retain the protein-producing nuclei they gained before.

Both passages are concerned with explaining muscle memory. However, while the author of passage A merely theorizes about neurons, muscle fibers, and mental explanations, the author of passage B presents scientific evidence regarding muscle cells, nuclei, and proteins.

1. (C) Global

Step 2: Identify the Question Type

The question asks for something both passages seek to answer. The correct answer will be based on the Scope and Purpose of both passages overall, making this a Global question.

Step 3: Research the Relevant Text

Because the correct answer will be based on the Scope and Purpose of the passages, there is no need to go back into the text itself.

Step 4: Make a Prediction

Both passages are focused on explanations for muscle memory, i.e., why people who have exercised before find it easier to build muscles the second time around.

Step 5: Evaluate the Answer Choices

(C) matches the main focus of both passages.

(A) brings up inconclusive explanations, which are not mentioned in passage B. Moreover, the author of passage A never actually explains *why* explanations are inconclusive.

(B) is a Distortion. Both passages focus on the effects of training, not on actual training methods or regimens.

(D) questions whether muscle memory is *psychological*, a concept only brought up in the last paragraph of passage A. Passage B does not address psychological explanations at all.

(E) also brings up *psychological* explanations, which is only addressed partially in passage A and never in passage B.

2. (B) Logic Reasoning (Method of Argument)

Step 2: Identify the Question Type

The word *by* indicates that the question is asking for *how* the author of passage B argues, making this a Method of Argument question similar to those found in Logical Reasoning.

Step 3: Research the Relevant Text

The question asks about the method used throughout passage B, so there's no specific text to research. Instead, because the question asks about how passage B differs from passage A, consider the relationship between the two passages.

Step 4: Make a Prediction

The difference between the passages is that passage B actually presents scientific evidence, while passage A merely presents unsupported theories. The correct answer will focus on passage B's use of scientific evidence.

Step 5: Evaluate the Answer Choices

(B) matches passage B's use of a scientific experiment (the one with mice), which contrasts the lack of scientific evidence in passage A.

(A) is a Distortion. The author of passage B provides evidence to explain the phenomenon of muscle memory. There is no questioning whether it's real or not.

(C) is a 180. Passage A addresses the reader personally (using the words *you* and *your*). Passage B refers to scientific evidence.

(D) is a 180. Passage A addresses psychological factors in the last paragraph. Passage B sticks to biological factors, including cells, nuclei, and proteins.

(E) is a 180. Passage A provides mere speculation. Passage B actually presents scientific evidence.

3. (A) Inference

Step 2: Identify the Question Type

The question asks for something passage B *suggests*, making this an Inference question.

Step 3: Research the Relevant Text

Because the entire passage revolves around muscle memory, everything is potentially relevant. However, the direct cause according to passage B is brought up at the very end. Start there and work backward.

Step 4: Make a Prediction

According to passage B, muscle memory is due to "extra nuclei" sticking around to make proteins (lines 58–61). This refers to the science in paragraph 2, in which muscle cells gain extra nuclei by merging with stem cells (lines 44–48). None of this is discussed in passage A, so the correct answer will revolve around this explanation.

Step 5: Evaluate the Answer Choices

(A) is correct, addressing the initial concept of muscle cells merging with stem cells.

(B) is a 180. Passage A does bring up the body's ability to adapt in lines 19–22.

(C) is a 180. Passage A brings up psychological factors in the third paragraph.

(D) is a Faulty Use of Detail. Passage B does bring up apoptosis (line 51), but that's part of the rejected assumption that extra nuclei die off. Muscle memory is based on the idea that those nuclei did *not* die off.

(E) is a 180. Passage A discusses neurons stimulating muscles in the second paragraph.

4. (C) Inference

Step 2: Identify the Question Type

The question directly asks for something that "can be inferred," making this an Inference question.

Step 3: Research the Relevant Text

There are no research clues, so the entire text is relevant. The question does ask about the author of passage A, but it mentions making an inference from the *passages*. So, both passages will be relevant.

Step 4: Make a Prediction

The question is far too open-ended to make a specific prediction. Just stick to the global ideas (passage A deals with unsupported theories while B offers a scientific explanation), and test the answers one at a time.

Step 5: Evaluate the Answer Choices

(C) is correct. The author of passage A claims that "virtually no discussions of [muscle memory] have appeared in scientific publications." Given that the two theories in passage A make no mention of the details from the research in passage B, the author of passage A is surely working without knowledge of that research.

(A) is a 180. Neither author questions the existence of muscle memory. They both equally admit it's real.

(B) is not supported, as the author of passage A makes no mention of any of the details raised by passage B. In fact, passage A raises the possibility of entirely different theories.

(D) is not supported. The author of passage A presents two theories as merely *potential* or *possible* explanations. There is no reason to believe that the author would be against a new theory if it's plausible.

(E) is not supported. The author of passage A never mentions other species at all, so there's no way to determine how that author would feel about using the study of mice to draw inferences about human muscles.

5. (D) Global

Step 2: Identify the Question Type

The question asks for the expected target audience of each passage. The correct answer will be based on each passage in its entirety, making this an unusual twist on a Global question.

Step 3: Research the Relevant Text

The answer will be based on the entire content of each passage, so there is no specific text to research.

Step 4: Make a Prediction

Both passages discuss explanations for muscle memory, but passage A makes consistent references to lifting weights (lines 13, 15, 22, 32–33) while passage B merely refers to exercise and muscle development in general. Thus, passage A definitely has a more specific target audience than passage B.

Step 5: Evaluate the Answer Choices

(D) matches passage A's more specific target audience: bodybuilders who lift weights.

(A) is flawed on both counts. Neither passage addresses any skepticism about muscle memory. Additionally, passage A, not passage B, addresses people with personal experience (using words such as *you* and *your*).

(B) is a Distortion on both counts. Passage A's puzzlement over the lack of scientific information might be motive to address researchers, but passage A never directly calls for action. Moreover, there's no reason to believe that passage B's scientific discussion is directed at coaches or trainers.

(C) is not supported. Neither passage draws a distinction between those working out alone and those working with a trainer, so neither group could be considered a target audience.

(E) is perhaps Half-Right, Half-Wrong because the science of passage B would probably be of interest to physiologists. However, passage A only brings up psychological ideas in the last paragraph. The entire second paragraph about neurons and muscle fibers would be irrelevant to psychologists.

6. (D) Inference

Step 2: Identify the Question Type

The question asks for a view the author of passage B would be "most likely to hold," making this an Inference question.

Step 3: Research the Relevant Text

The question directly refers to the first sentence of passage A. Start with that, and consider what content in passage B would address that claim.

Step 4: Make a Prediction

The first sentence of passage A characterizes muscle memory as a "puzzling phenomenon." This refers to that author's surprise about the lack of a scientific explanation. However, passage B actually brings up scientific research that could explain muscle memory. Thus, the author of passage B would suggest that muscle memory may not be as *puzzling* as passage A suggests.

Step 5: Evaluate the Answer Choices

(D) matches the idea that the scientific evidence makes muscle memory a less puzzling phenomenon.

(A) is a 180. The author of passage B does not deny the experiences of bodybuilders. In fact, passage B provides evidence that helps explain their experiences.

(B) is a 180. There is no dichotomy. What athletes experience is consistent with what passage B suggests happens at the cellular level.

(C) is unsupported. There's no information about what "most athletes" would believe. If they were unaware of the scientific evidence raised in passage B, they might be just as puzzled as the author of passage A.

(E) is a Distortion. Passage B never suggests that the author of passage A has any misunderstanding about anything, let alone "exercise psychology," a concept that passage B never mentions.

7. (E) Detail

Step 2: Identify the Question Type

The question asks for something "explicitly mentioned," making this a Detail question.

Step 3: Research the Relevant Text

The question provides no research clues, so the entire text is relevant.

Step 4: Make a Prediction

Passage B mentions many things that are never found in passage A, including muscle cell nuclei, proteins, stem cells, apoptosis, mice, and so on. If something doesn't jump out immediately in the answers, look for answers that can be eliminated because they *are* mentioned in passage A (e.g., neurons, muscle fibers).

Step 5: Evaluate the Answer Choices

(E) is correct. The need for protein is mentioned in lines 43–44, but never in passage A.

(A) is a 180. Passage A mentions such conditions in lines 23–26.

(B) is a 180. Passage A mentions muscles adapting in lines 19–22.

(C) is a 180. Passage A mentions muscle fiber percentage in line 21.

(D) is a 180. Passage A mentions discussion in scientific publications in lines 3–4.

Passage 2: Eileen Gray

Step 1: Read the Passage Strategically

Sample Roadmap

line #	Keyword/phrase	¶ Margin notes
1	Best known	E.G. career
2	fascinating	Studied lacquer:
3	:	layering
5	Though; shifted	simple aesthetics
6	always; even	
7	forever	
13	fit well	
14	eschewed	
16	preferring	
20	This tension	Tension b/w aesthetics and structure
23	critical; but; :	Led to interior design:
26	early; later	objects artistic and functional
30	:	
34	subsequently	
35	heavily invested	
39	though	
41	prefigures; did not believe	Led to architecture
46	:	structured house as whole
47	But	inside out
52	One such	no "exterior" or "interior"
55–56	no important distinction	

Discussion

The passage opens by introducing Eileen Gray, noting the years of her life span, and mentioning her "fascinating and multifaceted career." This makes Eileen Gray the **Topic** of this typical biography passage on the LSAT. Most biography passages are organized as a progression from one stage of the person's life or career to the next. The description of her artistic career (the **Scope** of the passage) in lines 3–4 foreshadows the structure of this passage: designing ornaments, then furniture, then interiors, and then homes. This common technique is great to notice as it offers an easy way to break down the remaining content.

Sure enough, the rest of the first paragraph discusses her work with lacquer, which applies to ornaments (bowls, screens) and furniture. The first sentence claimed she is best known for such work, and the author provides ample detail on this subject. Lacquering involves a series of layers, and the aesthetic result is austere ("straight lines and simple forms"), which veered from the showier style of the Art Nouveau movement of the time.

The second paragraph reveals more about her lacquer work, noting it's not just about aesthetics. There are also structural elements (e.g., lacquering properly to prevent the wood from warping), and both are critical to her work. The passage describes her applying this technique to various objects, creating pieces that were both artistic and functional. This *subsequently* (line 34) led to the next phase in her career: interior design. As with the lacquer objects, she created areas that were aesthetically stark, yet functional.

In the third paragraph, the author moves on to the final stage in Gray's career: architecture. Again, her principles from lacquering and interior design carry forward. Individual components were layered so as to allow for multiple functions. Nothing was "exterior" or "interior." Every part of the house was designed to function as a whole.

The author offers very little in the way of opinion, so the **Purpose** of this passage is merely to inform the reader about Gray's career. The **Main Idea** is that she had a varied career that carried forward her artistic principles of combining aesthetics and function and seeing everything as part of a whole.

8. (B) Global

Step 2: Identify the Question Type

The question asks for the "main point of the passage," making this a Global question.

Step 3: Research the Relevant Text

As with most Global questions, the entire text here is relevant. Instead of going back into the text, just consider the Main Point as predicted after reading the passage.

Step 4: Make a Prediction

The main point is very objective: Eileen Gray had a varied artistic career, taking the artistic principles from her work with lacquer and carrying them through to her work in architecture.

Step 5: Evaluate the Answer Choices

(B) is correct, identifying her varied career and how the aesthetic style she developed from her work with lacquer carried forward to her "everything works as a whole" style of architecture.

(A) starts off perfectly, but veers off at the end, suggesting she never received critical acclaim. The author never mentioned any critical reception, so this could not be part of the main point.

(C) contradicts the first sentence, which suggests she is best known for her work in lacquer, not her use of modern materials (a concept only presented tangentially in lines 37–39).

(D) is a Distortion. The author does mention *hidden* elements in some of Gray's work, but never claims this makes her work "readily identifiable."

(E) is a 180. Gray *embraced* the concept of integral wholeness, which she carried forward from her work in the Japanese tradition of lacquering. There is no dissatisfaction at all.

9. (E) Inference

Step 2: Identify the Question Type

The question asks for something that would exemplify the characteristics of Gray's work. Such an example will not be stated, but can be inferred based on the descriptions in the passage. This is a common Inference variation.

Step 3: Research the Relevant Text

The passage lists several characteristics of Gray's work. Some of the most prominent appear at the end of the first and second paragraphs.

Step 4: Make a Prediction

In describing Gray's work, the author notes Gray's preference for "straight lines and simple forms" (line 17). This austere quality is raised again in line 39, which also notes another frequently discussed characteristic: functionality. The correct answer should be an aesthetically simple creation that serves a functional purpose.

Step 5: Evaluate the Answer Choices

(E) matches Gray's style. The shape is described as simple, which matches Gray's aesthetic sensibility. It's made to fit the human form, which ensures it would be functional.

(A) is a 180. Tasseled fringes and curved arms go against Gray's preference for "straight lines and simple forms."

(B) is a 180. Gray prefers "straight lines and simple forms," not "intricate carvings" of wildlife.

(C) is a 180. While the functional aspect matches, the aesthetic style of mimicking "ornate flowers" does not.

(D) is not supported. The use of many different components (beads, pearls, and shells) does not fit Gray's simpler style.

10. (E) Inference

Step 2: Identify the Question Type

The correct answer will be supported by information in the passage, making this an Inference question.

Step 3: Research the Relevant Text

There are no research clues, so the entire text is relevant.

Step 4: Make a Prediction

It's difficult to predict an answer here; there are too many possible inferences. Instead, eliminate answers that are clearly beyond the Scope of the passage, and use content clues in the answer choices to do any necessary research.

Step 5: Evaluate the Answer Choices

(E) matches Gray's progression toward functionality, as noted in lines 37–39 and 49–52.

(A) is a 180. Any hint to Gray's reputation comes from the first sentence, which suggests that she *is* best known for a particular medium: her work with lacquer.

(B) is Extreme. The author mentions that she *often* created her own furniture (lines 36–38), but does not say she constructed *most* of the furnishings she designed.

(C) is a Distortion. The technique of lacquering was not common in Paris (lines 10–11), but there's no suggestion that artists didn't use wood or even found it *inappropriate*.

(D) is not supported. There's no suggestion that she withheld anything from public viewing.

11. (C) Detail

Step 2: Identify the Question Type

The correct answer will be a question that is directly answered in the passage. That means there will be a detail in the passage that corresponds to the correct answer.

Step 3: Research the Relevant Text

With no research clues, the entire text is relevant.

Step 4: Make a Prediction

The correct answer could refer to any detail from anywhere in the passage. The only approach is to test the answers one at a time, doing research when necessary to ensure there's a direct answer to the question provided.

Step 5: Evaluate the Answer Choices

(C) is directly answered in lines 13–17, which claim that the "straight lines and simple forms" of lacquering were *not* similar to the showier style of Art Nouveau.

(A) is not answered. It is only known that lacquer was "little known in Europe" during the early days of Gray's career, but there's no indication of when it was first introduced.

(B) is not answered. The passage mentions different types of wood surfaces (bowls, screens, furniture), but never mentions any specific types of wood.

(D) is not answered. In all the discussion of her architectural design, there is no mention of using the surrounding landscape.

(E) is not answered. The only materials mentioned are the wood used in lacquering and the steel used in some of her furniture. However, neither of those were said to be used for their structurally superior strength.

12. (A) Inference

Step 2: Identify the Question Type

The question asks for the "author's attitude" toward Gray's work, which is a common variation of an Inference question.

Step 3: Research the Relevant Text

The author's voice is noticeably lacking in this passage. Instead, the attitude will be gleaned from the overall tone of the passage.

Step 4: Make a Prediction

The sole indication of the author's attitude is the use of the word *fascinating* (line 2) to describe Gray's career. The rest of the passage describes her aesthetic style that carried forward through various stages in her career. The correct answer will be positive overall and will likely stay focused on her style.

Step 5: Evaluate the Answer Choices

(A) is consistent with the author's tone. The author spends the entire passage describing her aesthetic philosophy. The opening line indicates appreciation of Gray's *fascinating* career, and lines 13–17 indicate how her philosophy helped her eschew the flourishing style adapted by her contemporaries.

(B) is a Distortion. While Gray did eschew the flourishing Art Nouveau movement, the author never suggests she was pushed to the periphery for her independent ways.

(C) is not supported. While lacquering was a traditional Japanese technique, there's no mention of any Japanese "architectural traditions."

(D) is a Distortion. There's no indication that her career developed rapidly, and there's no indication she was recognized as an "avant-garde artist."

(E) is Extreme. She may have had her own style of architectural design, but it's never suggested that she *revolutionized* the field of structural design.

13. (B) Logic Reasoning (Principle)

Step 2: Identify the Question Type

The question asks for a principle used by Gray in her work, which means this works like a Principle question in Logical Reasoning.

Step 3: Research the Relevant Text

The principles invoked in Gray's work are described throughout the second and third paragraphs.

Step 4: Make a Prediction

Gray's work is frequently described as serving multiple functions (lines 32–34, 38–39, 49–52), which emphasizes the idea that things work together "as an integrated whole" (line 45). The correct answer will express this idea of individual items being part of a whole.

Step 5: Evaluate the Answer Choices

(B) matches Gray's style of using individual objects (interior features) to create an integrated whole (overall structural design).

(A) is not supported. The author only mentions the use of wood in lacquering. There's no indication of Gray's application of that technique to other materials.

(C) is a Distortion. Gray carried forward the aesthetic and structural principles behind lacquer, but there's no indication that the actual technique of lacquering would be suitable for large structural elements.

(D) is a 180. Gray preferred "straight lines and simple forms." She never expressed interested in mixing this with "ornate elements."

(E) is not supported. Gray's work is said to have involved "hidden layers" (line 48), which suggests that visual aspects would not necessarily give evidence of those unseen components.

14. (C) Inference

Step 2: Identify the Question Type

The question asks for something the passage *suggests* and that the author "would agree with," making this an Inference question.

Step 3: Research the Relevant Text

The question asks about Gray's architectural work, which is described in the third paragraph.

Step 4: Make a Prediction

The third paragraph mentions Gray's architectural style, which involves seeing interior and exterior elements as part of a unified whole, rather than as independent components. It talks about hidden layers and how Gray felt her architecture was similar to her work with lacquer.

Unfortunately, the correct answer to this question is not based on anything in the third paragraph. The correct answer is based on the very first sentence, a sentence that is worthy to note upon first reading the passage, but you wouldn't necessarily expect it to play a role in this question. On Test Day, it is vital that questions like these do not monopolize your time. Give them ample effort. Eliminate answers that are clearly wrong. However, know when it's time to move on. You never want to sacrifice an entire passage from later in the section, just for the sake of completing a single question.

Step 5: Evaluate the Answer Choices

(C) is the correct answer. The support from this comes from the very first line, which indicates that Gray is "best known for her work with lacquer." If that's what she's *best* known for, then she must be somewhat less known for everything else, including her work in architecture.

(A) is not supported. There is no mention of the views of any other architects.

(B) is a 180. There was no "radical shift" in her attitude. On the contrary, her architecture was based on the same attitudes she brought to her earlier work.

(D) is not supported. There is no mention of any of her work being controversial, so there is no basis for comparing her work on this quality.

(E) is a 180. Gray felt her architectural work was "like her work in lacquer" (line 46), which means they were similarly inspired by the Japanese tradition of layering.

Passage 3: Mesolithic Woodland Clearings

Step 1: Read the Passage Strategically

Sample Roadmap

line #	Keyword/phrase	¶ Margin notes
1	generally accepted	General view:
4	Whether	Mesolithic clearings used to get food
6	or whether	Auth: evidence not conclusive
7	common view	
9	however; at best; circumstantial	
13	but	
14	Furthermore	
17	generally lacking	
20	rather than	Some evidence supports
22	But	other evidence contradicts
23	while	
24	bolster	
25	may suggest a different vision	
28	argues	Tuan: humans fear wilderness
30	driven by; While	may apply to Mesolithic era
31	tempted	
32	clear	
33	If	
35	may change	
39	However	Auth: Mesolithic paths created due to fear
41	only recently; I propose	
46	alternative hypothesis	Alt view:
47	First	clearings developed where paths meet
48	Then	
51	legitimately consider	
54	finally	

Discussion

The passage opens with the **Topic**: woodland clearings. The prevailing view is that these clearings had an economic purpose: they provided a place to procure food. *However*, the author is not entirely convinced. The evidence provided is not conclusive, and there's no real evidence of animal preparation near the clearings.

The author's doubts continue in the second paragraph, in which the author bemoans the lack of archeological evidence and claims there's merely some ethnographic evidence. *But* the author is quick to point out that there is also ethnographic evidence that contradicts the prevailing view and points to *noneconomic* uses. At this point, it becomes clear that the **Scope** of the passage is determining the real purpose of the clearings.

In the third paragraph, the author suddenly digresses to introduce Yi-Fu Tuan, a geographer who talks about humans and their fear of wilderness. This seems off topic, but nothing is off topic in an LSAT passage. Sure enough, by the end of the paragraph, the author suggests this could shed light on the woodland clearings.

The author then discusses paths created by Mesolithic humans, who had a tendency to move around. The author hypothesizes that the paths were created due to the fear of wilderness, tying things back to Tuan's ideas. This leads to the final paragraph, in which the author's **Purpose** is clear: to present an alternative hypothesis about the clearings. As the paths became permanent and more frequently used, clearings emerged where the paths met, basically providing shortcuts and giving people a place to rest. So, the **Main Idea** is that, contrary to the view that clearings were used to procure food, the author believes they served a noneconomic purpose: they were just a place where people literally crossed paths.

15. (B) Global

Step 2: Identify the Question Type

The question asks for the "main idea" of the passage, making this a Global question.

Step 3: Research the Relevant Text

All of the text is relevant to this question. Instead, focus on the Main Idea of the passage, as discovered in Step 1.

Step 4: Make a Prediction

The main idea is that Mesolithic clearings may have had a noneconomic purpose, contrary to the prevailing view that they were used to procure food.

Step 5: Evaluate the Answer Choices

(B) correctly addresses the noneconomic theory as an alternative to the prevailing resource-procurement model.

(A) provides distorted information based on the wilderness discussion from the third and fourth paragraphs, but completely misses the author's focus on the Mesolithic woodland clearings.

(C) is Half-Right, Half-Wrong. It correctly notes the existence of ethnographic evidence in favor of the resource-procurement model. However, the author's point is not that there were "multiple purposes." The author's view is that there was a different noneconomic purpose, for which there is no archaeological evidence given.

(D) focuses on the wrong details (movement along paths instead of the woodland clearings). Besides, the idea of moving along paths is said to be a *fact* (line 39), not a hypothesis.

(E) is a 180 of information in the second paragraph. Instead of providing a clear explanation, some evidence supports one view while other evidence supports a conflicting view.

16. (B) Detail

Step 2: Identify the Question Type

"According to" suggests that the correct answer will be directly found in the text, making this a Detail question.

Step 3: Research the Relevant Text

The resource-procurement model is described primarily in the first paragraph.

Step 4: Make a Prediction

It's frequently called the "resource-procurement model," but the first sentence is more direct about the "resource" being procured: food. And the food in question is animals, which are either attracted to open areas or just easier to hunt when out in the open. Either way, the view is that animals entered the clearing to graze, and humans hunted them there for food.

Step 5: Evaluate the Answer Choices

(B) matches the stated view.

(A) is a Faulty Use of Detail. Pathways are part of the author's theory, not the resource-procurement model.

(C) is a Distortion. The potential use of the clearings was to attract presumably *wild* animals to be hunted, not to provide *domesticated* animals with a place to graze.

(D) is a Faulty Use of Detail. This is part of the author's theory in the final paragraph, not the resource-procurement model.

(E) mentions crops, which were never mentioned in the passage, let alone as part of the resource-procurement model.

17. (E) Logic Reasoning (Strengthen)

Step 2: Identify the Question Type

The question asks for information that "would lend support to the author's proposal," making this a Strengthen question like the ones found in Logical Reasoning.

Step 3: Research the Relevant Text

The question directly refers to the author's proposal in the next-to-last paragraph, which can be readily spotted by the phrase "I propose" (line 41).

Step 4: Make a Prediction

The author's proposal in the second-to-last paragraph is that the paths were created due to fear of the surrounding woodland. This is all based on Tuan's theory that humans fear wilderness. The author assumes that human actions (e.g., creating paths) can be motivated by the fears they have. The correct answer will strengthen that assumption by showing how people's actions can be based on their fears.

Step 5: Evaluate the Answer Choices

(E) strengthens the argument by showing how some premodern populations perform other actions (rituals) as protection from the wilderness they fear. If their fear motivates the performance of such rituals, then it's more likely that Mesolithic populations also had similar fears that motivated their creation of the paths.

(A) would not strengthen the author's proposal. It may help confirm that Mesolithic people used those paths and clearings, but offers no support that fear of wilderness was a motivator.

(B) would not strengthen the proposal. This would merely suggest that the paths were created in response to population density, not to any fear of wilderness.

(C) is irrelevant. Whether modern people use the paths offers no evidence why they were created in the first place or whether fear played any role in their creation.

(D) offers no help. This merely confirms Tuan's theory that people fear wilderness, but does not confirm that such fear was the motivator for building the paths.

18. (D) Inference

Step 2: Identify the Question Type

The question asks for something the author *suggests*, making this an Inference question.

Step 3: Research the Relevant Text

The author discusses the Mesolithic humans throughout the passage. However, the question asks what the *author* suggests and for something that *may* have been true. That suggests that the question refers to the author's theories in the last two paragraphs.

Step 4: Make a Prediction

At the end of the fourth paragraph and into the fifth passage, the author suggests that Mesolithic humans may have created paths out of fear of the wilderness (lines 41–45, 51–52) and that they created clearings for social purposes (lines 54–58).

Step 5: Evaluate the Answer Choices

(D) is supported, especially considering the author's theory that "wilderness [was] a motivating concept in the Mesolithic" (line 52).

(A) is Extreme. The author mentions this use of fire in line 22, but never suggests that Mesolithic humans were "the first" to do so.

(B) is Extreme. They used paths, but the author never claims or suggests that they were the *first* people to do so.

(C) is not supported. In fact, it is suggested that they feared nature (lines 42–45).

(E) is not supported. The only economic idea presented is the resource-procurement theory of using open clearings for hunting—hardly a "complex system."

19. (D) Logic Function

Step 2: Identify the Question Type

The phrase "in order to" indicates that the question is asking *why* the author mentions Tuan's argument, making this a Logic Function question.

Step 3: Research the Relevant Text

Tuan's argument, as the question indicates, is in the third paragraph. Be sure to consider how Tuan's argument fits within the context of the paragraph as well as the passage as a whole.

Step 4: Make a Prediction

Tuan's argument is about human fear of wilderness, an odd concept in a passage about wilderness clearings. However, the last sentence of the third paragraph indicates how this fits into the author's discussion. The author claims that applying Tuan's argument to the Mesolithic era can provide a new perspective on the woodland clearings (lines 33–35). The author then goes on to use Tuan's ideas as a basis for a new hypothesis about those clearings. And that's the true function of Tuan's argument in this passage.

Step 5: Evaluate the Answer Choices

(D) matches the prediction of Tuan's theory as a basis (groundwork) for the author's new hypothesis.

(A) is a Distortion. Tuan's theory merely supports the author's hypothesis. It is irrelevant to the generally accepted view, and thus has no effect (i.e., casts no doubt) on that theory.

(B) is a 180. Tuan's argument is the basis for the author's argument, not the hypothesis the author is challenging.

(C) is a Distortion. Tuan's argument is used as the basis for the *author's* hypothesis about clearings. Tuan himself offered no hypothesis on the clearings.

(E) is unsupported. Tuan's view is solely about human fear of wilderness. He is not said to hold any view about the Mesolithic clearings.

20. (A) Inference

Step 2: Identify the Question Type

The question asks for something that can be *inferred*, making this an Inference question.

Step 3: Research the Relevant Text

The question refers to the author's reluctance to accept the resource-procurement model. The author's misgivings are primarily laid out in the first paragraph.

Step 4: Make a Prediction

The author currently does not accept the resource-procurement model for two reasons. First, the author cites any existing evidence as "at best circumstantial" (line 9), suggesting there's no strong link between human artifacts and the clearings. Second, the author cites a lack of evidence "that preparation of animals for human consumption took place within or near such clearings" (lines 14–17). So, the author would be more likely to accept the theory if there was a stronger link between human artifacts and the clearings or if there was evidence of animal preparation near the clearings.

Step 5: Evaluate the Answer Choices

(A) is correct, as it would directly address the author's concern in lines 14–17.

(B) would be irrelevant. The author already admits that there is such evidence (lines 18–20), so such evidence has already done nothing to sway the author.

(C) would not help. The author never questions whether clearings would attract animals. Such experimental evidence would not do anything to address the author's stated concerns: the weak link between artifacts and clearings and the lack of evidence of animal preparation near the clearing.

(D) is a 180. This would suggest that the clearings were natural and not man-made, making the resource-procurement model look even *less* likely.

(E) is irrelevant. The number of clearings would offer no evidence on *why* they were created in the first place.

21. (A) Inference

Step 2: Identify the Question Type

The question asks for the closest meaning of a phrase the author uses. The meaning will not be stated directly, but will be an inference based on the context.

Step 3: Research the Relevant Text

The question directly refers to line 55, but be sure to read around that line and consider how that line fits within the context of the author's purpose.

Step 4: Make a Prediction

In line 55, the phrase "purely social phenomena" refers to the clearings described throughout the passage. This phrase is applied in the last paragraph, which describes the author's "alternative hypothesis," the one that contradicts the economic resource-procurement model. So, the phrase "purely social" indicates an entirely social basis for the clearings as opposed to an economic, food-based motivation.

Step 5: Evaluate the Answer Choices

(A) matches the author's idea that clearings arose because of noneconomic practices (the creation of paths due to the fear of wilderness).

(B) is not supported. There's no suggestion that clearings are universal (i.e., all societies create them), nor that they are unique to humans.

(C) is not supported. The idea of cutting corners and creating resting spots could very well be self-serving and have no intention of strengthening societal ties.

(D) is a Distortion. There may have been some social benefit (the clearings offered a place to rest and protection from the scary wilderness), but the author suggests that clearings merely *emerged* where paths crossed. There's no suggestion that the clearings were "intentionally created" to produce those benefits.

(E) is, at least in part, a 180. It may reveal cultural information, but the view being presented is a purely *noneconomic* one.

22. (E) Logic Reasoning (Parallel Reasoning)

Step 2: Identify the Question Type

The question asks for an argument "analogous to" another argument, making this a Parallel Reasoning question like those found in Logical Reasoning.

Step 3: Research the Relevant Text

The question directly points to the author's argument in the second paragraph.

Step 4: Make a Prediction

The author's argument in the second paragraph is that, while there may be ethnographic evidence that supports the resource-procurement model, there is other ethnographic evidence that "may suggest a different vision" (line 25). The correct answer will provide the same logic about a completely different topic: there is some type of evidence that supports one point of view, but there is other evidence of the same type that supports a different view.

Step 5: Evaluate the Answer Choices

(E) matches the logic. As with the author's argument, this presents a particular type of evidence (circumstantial evidence), of which there is some that supports one view (the defendant is guilty) and some that supports a different view (the defendant is innocent).

(A) is Half-Right, Half-Wrong. This correctly suggests that one type of evidence (circumstantial) supports one view, but there's another type (direct) that *establishes* another view. Not only are there not two different types of evidence in the passage, but the author's second set of evidence never *established* anything. Both sets of evidence in the original merely supported or suggested a point of view.

(B) does not match. Unlike the original argument, this uses the exact same evidence to arrive at two different conclusions, suggesting a difference in interpretation. The original argument presented evidence of the same *type*, but entirely different (*other*) evidence to support a different view.

(C) is Extreme and a Distortion. It may be tempting for those who concentrated on the author's claim that *most* evidence was from "ethnography rather than archaeology." However, the original argument never suggests that the evidence is *entirely* ethnographic, with *no* archaeological evidence. This answer is far too strong, and it also ignores the counterevidence raised in the second half of the paragraph.

(D) does not match. This brings up the concepts of trustworthiness and reliability, which do not logically compare to the original argument.

Passage 4: Specific Performance

Step 1: Read the Passage Strategically

Sample Roadmap

line #	Keyword/phrase	¶ Margin notes
9	But; while	Specific performance
10	better	Auth: sometimes good, sometimes not
11	alternative	
12	clearly not; suitable	
14	depends on	SP good when $ not enough
15	only	Ex.
16	reasonable	
18	For example	
24	best	
27	Nevertheless	When $ not enough
29	thus	SP can be bad
30	In fact	Ex. employment
32	detrimental	can cause friction
33	thus; should be avoided	$ would be better
37	especially if	
39	most compelling	
43	especially	
45	heighten dissatisfaction; intensify	
46	friction; Even if	
49	do better to avoid; uncomfortable	
51	permits; steer clear	
52	troublesome	
53	while	

Discussion

In the first paragraph, the author introduces "specific performance" (**Topic**), a court ruling applied in some breach of contract disputes. With specific performance, the person who violated the contract is simply ordered to do what was promised in the first place. No monetary damages are awarded. *But* the author argues that specific performance is only better than paying monetary damages in some cases. In other cases, specific performance would not be better. This is effectively the **Main Idea** of the passage. The rest of the passage merely goes into details and examples supporting this point. That makes the relative appropriateness of specific performance the **Scope**, with the **Purpose** being to describe instances when specific performance is more appropriate than monetary damages and when it's not.

The second paragraph describes when specific performance would be better. In general, it's when money wouldn't be adequate. As an example, the author cites a situation in which a seller backs out of a deal and won't sell a subjectively important object (i.e., something of personal value). In that case, the court would simply order the seller to sell the item as promised for the agreed-upon price.

The third paragraph focuses on cases when money *would* be adequate. In those cases, the author argues that specific performance would be a bad idea. As an example, the author mentions contracts involving a service to be performed (e.g., construction work). In such cases, it would be harder for courts to enforce specific performance, and it could lead to unsatisfactory service and psychological friction between parties. Monetary compensation would be a better solution.

23. (B) Logic Reasoning (Principle)

Step 2: Identify the Question Type

The correct answer will be a specific example that conforms to the general description of specific performance, as described in the passage. Finding a specific situation that conforms to a general rule is the hallmark of Principle questions, like those found in Logical Reasoning.

Step 3: Research the Relevant Text

The general description of specific performance is provided in the first paragraph.

Step 4: Make a Prediction

Specific performance is defined clearly in the first sentence (lines 1–4): compelling participants to do precisely what they agreed to do. The correct answer will provide a specific example in which there was an agreement, and all parties involved are ordered to honor the agreement.

Step 5: Evaluate the Answer Choices

(B) matches the concept perfectly. Both the analyst and the company are ordered to do what they agreed upon in the first place: the analyst is ordered to do her promised work, and the company is ordered to pay the salary it promised.

(A) does not match. In this case, the contract is simply thrown out. Nobody is made to follow through on the original agreement.

(C) does not match. Instead of ordering the contractor to fulfill the agreement, this orders the contractor to pass the burden on to somebody else.

(D) does not match. There was no breach of contract. The buyer paid for the item, and the seller provided the item. The contract was fulfilled. The question of the item's authenticity is another matter altogether.

(E) does not match. This involves awarding monetary damages, which is what specific performance is meant to avoid. Also, the engineer is not ordered to fulfill the contract, which is what specific performance is all about.

24. (C) Inference

Step 2: Identify the Question Type

The question asks for something the author would "most likely agree with," "[b]ased on the passage." That makes this an Inference question.

Step 3: Research the Relevant Text

The question asks about a situation in which someone failed to undertake employment as contracted, a concept raised in lines 38–39.

Step 4: Make a Prediction

Within the context of lines 30–39, someone refusing to undertake employment is an example of when specific performance "would actually be detrimental to those involved in the dispute and thus should be avoided."

Step 5: Evaluate the Answer Choices

(C) is supported, as the situation in the question stem fits exactly the kind of circumstance described throughout the third paragraph, which identifies when monetary damages can be superior to specific performance.

(A) is a 180. The author claims specific performance can be *detrimental*, not helpful, in such a case.

(B) is a Distortion. While the author might agree with weighing monetary factors against psychological concerns, the author already categorizes breach of employment contracts as unsuited to specific performance. Moreover, there is no indication that specific performance costs the courts less. In fact, lines 46–48 suggest otherwise.

(D) is not supported. Even under such dire circumstances, the author claims that specific performance can be *detrimental* in such cases. There is no suggestion that the author would support it as a plan B. Perhaps there are other solutions not raised in the passage.

(E) is an Irrelevant Comparison. It is only claimed in the first sentence that courts "sometimes use" specific performance. The author argues when it *should* be used, but there's no indication of the situations in which it actually *is* used more often.

25. (E) Global

Step 2: Identify the Question Type

The question asks for the "main purpose" of the entire passage, making this a Global question.

Step 3: Research the Relevant Text

Because the question asks about the passage as a whole, the entire text is relevant. Instead, use the Purpose as predicted in Step 1.

Step 4: Make a Prediction

The author claims that specific performance can be better than monetary damages in some cases, but not in others (lines 9–12). The rest of the passage merely provides examples of when one solution is better and when the other is better. That's the author's purpose.

Step 5: Evaluate the Answer Choices

(E) is correct. The author identifies situations for assessing the relative applicability of two remedies: specific performance vs. monetary damages.

(A) is a Distortion. The author never suggests that specific performance will become a "standard approach." It is merely used *sometimes*.

(B) is a Distortion. The author provides a few examples, but never offers a full "set of standards" and never argues for implementation of those standards. Also, there's no indication that specific performance is a "new legal measure."

(C) is a Distortion. The author does describe some differences between specific performance and monetary damages, but this completely ignores the author's focus on determining which solution is more applicable in certain situations.

(D) brings up evidence in contract disputes, which the author never addresses, let alone provides any guidelines for evaluating.

26. (A) Inference

Step 2: Identify the Question Type

The question asks for something the passage "strongly suggests" that the "author would agree with," making this an Inference question.

Step 3: Research the Relevant Text

With no research clues, the entire text is relevant.

Step 4: Make a Prediction

With no clues for reference, stay focused on the big picture: the author never conclusively supports monetary damages or specific performance. It all depends on whether monetary factors are adequate or not. Start with this global theme, eliminate answers that are clearly wrong, and use content clues in the answer choices to do any necessary research.

Step 5: Evaluate the Answer Choices

(A) is correct, fitting the consistent theme of the passage. The author states that specific performance would be acceptable when "monetary damages could not adequately compensate" (lines 15–18). When monetary damages *could* compensate, the court "need not consider ordering specific performance" (lines 27–30). That suggests that assessing monetary damages is a key consideration.

(B) is not supported. The author claims specific performance is reasonable for contracts selling personal property "that is unique or of such subjective importance to the buyer." However, those could be rare instances and not *usually* be the case with sales of personal property in general.

(C) is Extreme. This basically dismisses specific performance entirely, but the author admits that there are cases in which specific performance is an acceptable alternative (lines 9–12, 15–18).

(D) is an Extreme Distortion. The author cites specific performance as useful in circumstances when items have "subjective importance." However, that does not mean the objective value is low. Items can be both subjectively and objectively valuable. Besides, the author does not suggest that these are the *only* disputes in which specific performance would be successful.

(E) is not supported. The author cites examples in which one method would be more suitable than another. However, the author never suggests *offering* disputing parties the option to choose which one they'd prefer.

27. (C) Logic Reasoning (Strengthen)

Step 2: Identify the Question Type

The question asks for something that would "strengthen the author's position," which makes this a Strengthen question like those in Logical Reasoning.

Step 3: Research the Relevant Text

The question refers to "employment contract cases," which are brought up in lines 37–39.

Step 4: Make a Prediction

In the third paragraph, the author cites employment contract cases as an example of ones in which monetary damages would be more effective than specific performance. In other words, it would be better to order violating parties to just pay companies money rather than complete the work they promised. The correct answer will validate that awarding monetary damages will be a more effective solution.

Step 5: Evaluate the Answer Choices

(C) strengthens the author's recommendation. If the people violating these contracts couldn't afford the monetary damages, then companies would get no service *and* no money. It's important that people have enough money to pay the damages.

(A) is a 180. If such compensation is hard to enforce, then it looks *less* warranted to make that recommendation.

(B) is a 180, at worst. If all remedies, including monetary compensation, involved coercion, then dissatisfaction and friction could be involved in any case. That does not make monetary compensation look any better.

(D) is a possible 180. The author claims monetary damages are better, in general, for breaches of service contracts (lines 30–36). If employment cases are very different, that may suggest monetary damages are *not* better in those cases.

(E) is a 180. This suggests that employee rights are more important than monetary considerations, contradicting the author's recommendation to award monetary damages.

Section III: Logic Games

Game 1: Bookmobile

Q#	Question Type	Correct	Difficulty
1	Acceptability	B	★
2	Must Be False (CANNOT Be True)	C	★
3	"If" / Must Be True	A	★
4	"If" / Must Be True	B	★
5	"If" / Must Be True	D	★

Game 2: National Park Rangers

Q#	Question Type	Correct	Difficulty
6	Acceptability	E	★
7	"If" / Could Be True	C	★
8	"If" / Must Be True	D	★★
9	Must Be False (CANNOT Be True)	D	★
10	"If" / Could Be True	E	★★
11	"If" / Could Be True	B	★★
12	"If" / Must Be True	A	★★

Game 3: Economic TAs

Q#	Question Type	Correct	Difficulty
13	Partial Acceptability	A	★
14	Partial Acceptability (CANNOT)	B	★★
15	Could Be True	A	★
16	"If" / Must Be False (CANNOT Be True)	C	★★
17	"If" / Must Be True	D	★★★★

Game 4: Computer Virus

Q#	Question Type	Correct	Difficulty
18	Partial Acceptability	D	★★
19	Could Be True	E	★★
20	"If" / Must Be True	A	★★★
21	Could Be True EXCEPT	C	★★★
22	Completely Determine	C	★★★
23	"If" / Must Be True	C	★★★

Game 1: Bookmobile

Step 1: Overview

Situation: A bookmobile visiting various neighborhoods

Entities: Six neighborhoods (Hidden Hills, Lakeville, Nottingham, Oldtown, Park Plaza, Sunnyside)

Action: Selection/Sequencing Hybrid. Determine which five neighborhoods will be visited (Selection) and the order in which they will be visited (Sequencing).

Limitations: Exactly five neighborhoods will be visited, one per day, with no neighborhood being visited more than once.

Step 2: Sketch

List the neighborhoods by initial. (For simplicity, use a single initial for the two-word neighborhoods, e.g., H for Hidden Hills). For the selection, write "5/6" next to the entities. As the game proceeds, circle neighborhoods that are selected and cross out the one that isn't. For the sequencing, draw five slots labeled with each day of the week, Monday through Friday.

H L N O P S – Pick 5 of 6

$$\overline{\text{Mo}} \ \overline{\text{Tu}} \ \overline{\text{We}} \ \overline{\text{Th}} \ \overline{\text{Fr}}$$

Step 3: Rules

Rule 1 provides two pieces of information. Hidden Hills is visited, so circle H in the entity list. However, it's not visited on Friday, so draw "~ H" under Friday.

Rule 2 presents some Formal Logic. If Oldtown is visited, then it must be visited immediately before Hidden Hills.

$$O \rightarrow \underline{O} \ \underline{H}$$

The contrapositive for a rule like this is awkward, so this is a rare case in which a contrapositive is not needed (or, in this particular case, not really helpful).

Rule 3 is more Formal Logic. If Lakeville is visited, it must be visited on Wednesday. So, by contrapositive, if Lakeville is not visited on Wednesday, it's not visited at all:

$$L \rightarrow \frac{L}{We}$$

$$\sim \frac{L}{We} \rightarrow \sim L$$

Rule 4 provides two pieces of information. First, Nottingham and Sunnyside are both visited, so circle N and S in the entity list. However, they cannot be visited consecutively, so make a shorthand note of this.

$$\frac{N \ \ S}{S \ \ N}$$

Step 4: Deductions

The only potential Block of Entities is Oldtown and Hidden Hills (Rule 2), but that only exists *if* Oldtown is even visited. Moreover, even if it is, there are multiple possible outcomes.

However, it is useful to note that, if Oldtown is visited, it could not be visited on Friday. It also could not be visited on Thursday because Hidden Hills cannot be visited on Friday (Rule 1).

Rule 3 offers an opportunity for Limited Options. If Lakeville is visited, Rule 3 establishes it on Wednesday. If Lakeville is not visited, it will be the one neighborhood that is not visited. That means every other neighborhood would be. It's worth taking a moment to draw out both options.

In the first option, Lakeville is visited, and it is visited on Wednesday. Hidden Hills is also visited (Rule 1), as are Nottingham and Sunnyside (Rule 4). That leaves room for one more neighborhood. If it were Oldtown, that would create a block of Oldtown immediately before Hidden Hills (Rule 2). That block could not be placed on Thursday and Friday (Rule 1), and placing it on Monday and Tuesday would force Nottingham and Sunnyside to be consecutive, violating Rule 4. Therefore, Oldtown is not visited, making Park Plaza the fifth neighborhood. The selection is complete, but the order is still uncertain.

I) Ⓗ Ⓛ Ⓝ O̶ Ⓟ Ⓢ

$$\overline{\text{Mo}} \ \overline{\text{Tu}} \ \underset{L}{\overline{\text{We}}} \ \overline{\text{Th}} \ \underset{\sim H}{\overline{\text{Fr}}}$$

In the second option, Lakeville is not visited. That means all of the other neighborhoods are. With Oldtown visited, it must be visited immediately before Hidden Hills (Rule 2). That means Oldtown could not be visited on Friday, and Hidden Hills could not be visited on Monday. Further, Oldtown cannot be Thursday, as Hidden Hills cannot be visited on Friday (Rule 1). Again, the selection is complete, although the sequencing is still very open-ended.

II) Ⓗ L̶ Ⓝ Ⓞ Ⓟ Ⓢ

$$\underset{\sim H}{\overline{\text{Mo}}} \ \overline{\text{Tu}} \ \overline{\text{We}} \ \underset{\sim O}{\overline{\text{Th}}} \ \underset{\substack{\sim H \\ \sim O}}{\overline{\text{Fr}}}$$

The one other thing to potentially note is that Park Plaza is not mentioned in the rules, so it is the game's sole Floater.

Step 5: Questions

1. (B) Acceptability

As with any Acceptability question, use the rules one at a time to eliminate answers that violate those rules.

(E) violates Rule 1 by having Hidden Hills visited on Friday. **(D)** violates Rule 2 by having Oldtown visited, but not immediately before Hidden Hills. **(A)** violates Rule 3 by having Lakeville visited on Tuesday. **(C)** violates Rule 4 by having Nottingham and Sunnyside visited consecutively. That leaves **(B)** as the correct answer.

2. (C) Must Be False (CANNOT Be True)

The correct answer will be the neighborhood that cannot be visited on Thursday. The remaining answers will list neighborhoods that *could* be visited on Thursday.

Lakeville can only be visited on Wednesday, but is not listed in the answers. By Rule 2, if Oldtown is visited, it must be on the day before Hidden Hills is visited. Because Hidden Hills cannot be visited on Friday (Rule 1), Oldtown cannot be visited on Thursday. That makes **(C)** the correct answer.

3. (A) "If" / Must Be True

For this question, Hidden Hills is visited on Monday.

$$\frac{H}{Mo} \quad \frac{}{Tu} \quad \frac{}{We} \quad \frac{}{Th} \quad \frac{}{Fr}$$

That means Oldtown cannot be visited (Rule 2), so all other neighborhoods will be visited—as seen in Option I. That means Lakeville must be visited on Wednesday (Rule 3), which makes **(A)** the correct answer. The remaining answers are all possible, but need not be true.

4. (B) "If" / Must Be True

For this question, Hidden Hills is visited on Wednesday. That means Lakeville cannot be visited (Rule 3), which means all of the other neighborhoods are visited—as seen in Option II. Because Oldtown is visited, it must be visited the day before Hidden Hills, i.e., on Tuesday.

$$\frac{}{Mo} \quad \frac{O}{Tu} \quad \frac{H}{We} \quad \frac{}{Th} \quad \frac{}{Fr}$$

That makes **(B)** the correct answer. The remaining answers are all possible, but need not be true.

5. (D) "If" / Must Be True

For this question, Nottingham is visited on Thursday. That could happen in either of the two Limited Options, so test them both.

If Lakeville is visited (Option I), it will be visited on Wednesday. Friday cannot be the day the bookmobile visits Hidden Hills (Rule 1) or Sunnyside (Rule 4), so it must visit Park Plaza on Friday (Oldtown is not visited in Option I). Hidden Hills must be visited (Rule 1), as must Sunnyside (Rule 4). So, they will be visited on Monday and Tuesday in this option, in either order.

I) Ⓗ Ⓛ Ⓝ Ø Ⓟ Ⓢ
$$\frac{H/S}{Mo} \quad \frac{S/H}{Tu} \quad \frac{L}{We} \quad \frac{N}{Th} \quad \frac{P}{Fr}$$

If Lakeville is not visited, every other neighborhood is. Friday cannot be the day the bookmobile visits Hidden Hills (Rule 1), Oldtown (Rule 2), or Sunnyside (Rule 4), so it must visit Park Plaza on Friday. Oldtown must be visited the day before Hidden Hills (Rule 2). The New-"If" already placed Nottingham on Thursday, so Sunnyside cannot be visited on Wednesday (Rule 4). Thus, Sunnyside must be on Monday,

with Oldtown and Hidden Hills on Tuesday and Wednesday, respectively.

II) Ⓗ Ł Ⓝ Ⓞ Ⓟ Ⓢ
$$\frac{S}{Mo} \quad \frac{O}{Tu} \quad \frac{H}{We} \quad \frac{N}{Th} \quad \frac{P}{Fr}$$

In either case, Park Plaza is visited on Friday, making **(D)** the correct answer. The remaining answers are merely possible in just one option, or not possible at all.

Game 2: National Park Rangers

Step 1: Overview

Situation: Park rangers monitoring areas in a national park

Entities: Six rangers (Jefferson, Koguchi, Larson, Mendez, Olsen, Pruitt) and three areas (1, 2, 3)

Action: Distribution. Determine the area to which each ranger is assigned.

Limitations: Each ranger will be assigned to exactly one area. Each area will receive at least one but no more than three rangers.

Step 2: Sketch

List the rangers by initial and set up a chart with three columns, one for each area. Because each area gets at least one ranger, add one space to each area. The remaining spaces will be filled in as the game proceeds.

J K L M O P

1   2   3   (1-3 each)

Step 3: Rules

Rule 1 assigns Mendez to area 3. Add "M" to column 3, but leave the column open. Other rangers could still be assigned to that area.

Rule 2 prevents Olsen and Pruitt from being assigned to area 1. Draw "~ O" and "~ P" under column 1.

Rule 3 provides two possible blocks: Larson with Koguchi or Larson with Mendez. However, the rule also prevents those blocks from being together. So, draw the two options off to the side, but also note that they cannot all be together.

L   L
K or M

L
K
M

Rule 4 provides two pieces of Formal Logic. If Olsen is assigned to area 2, Jefferson and Koguchi will be assigned to the same area. Otherwise (i.e., if Olsen is *not* assigned to area 2), Jefferson and Koguchi are *not* together. You can draw these notes to the side in shorthand. However, this rule presents Limited Options, and it's more valuable to draw two sketches and build this rule directly into those options.

Step 4: Deductions

Using the fourth rule, draw two sketches, making sure they both include Mendez in area 3 (Rule 1). In the first option, Olsen will be assigned to area 2. In the second option, Olsen will *not* be assigned to area 2.

In the first option, with Olsen in area 2, Jefferson and Koguchi will be together. They cannot be assigned to area 3 because

that would put Koguchi with Mendez. Larson then couldn't be paired with Koguchi or Mendez without being assigned with both of them, violating Rule 3. The Jefferson-Koguchi block also cannot be assigned to area 2. That would leave only Larson and Pruitt available for area 1. However, Pruitt cannot be in area 1 (Rule 2), and Larson cannot be alone (Rule 3). So, Jefferson and Koguchi must be assigned to area 1. That leaves Larson and Pruitt. Larson has to be with Koguchi or Mendez, so Larson will be in area 1 or 3 (but not 2). And Pruitt cannot be in area 1, so Pruitt will be in area 2 or 3.

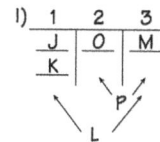

I)   1   2   3
     J   O   M
     K

          P

     L

In the second option, with Olsen *not* in area 2, Jefferson and Koguchi will be split, but could still go anywhere. Olsen, however, cannot be in area 1 (Rule 2), so Olsen would have to be in area 3. With Mendez already there, that leaves room for just one more ranger (there doesn't *have* to be a third ranger in area 3, but there cannot be any more). If there were a third ranger, it could be anybody except for Koguchi. Placing Koguchi in area 3 would prevent Larson from being paired with Koguchi or Mendez, thus violating Rule 3. Therefore, Koguchi must be assigned to area 1 or 2.

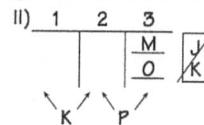

II)   1   2   3
                M   J
                O   K

           K   P

Step 5: Questions

6. (E) Acceptability

As with any Acceptability question, go through the rules one at a time, eliminating answers that violate those rules.

(D) violates Rule 1 by assigning Mendez to area 2. **(C)** violates Rule 2 by assigning Pruitt to area 1. **(A)** violates Rule 3 by assigning Larson to an area without Mendez or Koguchi. **(B)** violates Rule 4 by assigning Olsen to area 2, but not having Jefferson and Koguchi together. That leaves **(E)** as the correct answer.

7. (C) "If" / Could Be True

For this question, Olsen will be the only ranger assigned to area 2—that can only happen in Option I. As detailed in the deductions for Option I, by Rule 4, Jefferson and Koguchi will be together. They cannot be assigned with Mendez in area 3 without violating Rule 3, so they must be assigned to area 1. Pruitt cannot be assigned to area 1 (Rule 2). If Olsen is alone in area 2, Pruitt would have to be assigned to area 3. That leaves Larson, who can be assigned along with Koguchi in area 1 or Mendez in area 3.

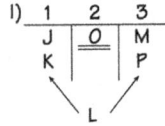

I)
```
   1   2   3
   J   O   M
   K       P
        \ L /
```

The question asks for a possible complete assignment to area 3. Area 3 must include Mendez and Pruitt. That eliminates **(A)**, **(B)**, and **(D)**. There is room for one more, but only Larson is available. That eliminates **(E)**. If Larson is assigned to area 1, then area 3 could just be Mendez and Pruitt, making **(C)** the correct answer.

8. (D) "If" / Must Be True

For this question, exactly one ranger will be assigned to area 1. It cannot be Larson (Rule 3), Mendez (Rule 1), Olsen (Rule 2), or Pruitt (Rule 2). That leaves Jefferson or Koguchi. That means they will be split up, so Olsen cannot be assigned to area 2 (Rule 4). That means Olsen must be assigned to area 3 with Mendez, making **(D)** the correct answer. The remaining answers are all possible, but need not be true.

This question can be answered quickly with the Limited Options as well. If exactly one ranger will be assigned to area 1, you must use Option II (because Jefferson and Koguchi are both in area 1 in Option I). The only ranger that was established by the deductions for Option II is Olsen in area 3, and sure enough, that matches **(D)**.

9. (D) Must Be False (CANNOT Be True)

The correct answer will be a ranger who cannot be assigned to area 3. The remaining four answers will list rangers who could be assigned to area 3.

Area 3 must include Mendez (Rule 1). Placing Koguchi in area 3 would prevent Larson from being assigned with only Mendez or Koguchi (not both), violating Rule 3. So, Koguchi cannot be assigned to area 3, making **(D)** the correct answer. The remaining rangers all *could* be assigned to area 3, even if they don't *need* to be.

10. (E) "If" / Could Be True

For this question, Koguchi is assigned to area 2. In that case, Olsen cannot also be assigned to area 2. Otherwise, Jefferson would be with Koguchi, too (Rule 4). However, that would leave nobody for area 1 because Pruitt cannot be in area 1 (Rule 1), and Larson cannot be alone (Rule 3). This was seen as impossible in Option I, so Olsen must be in area 3, as Option II shows. That leaves Jefferson, Larson, and Pruitt. Larson must be with Koguchi or Mendez, so Larson can only be in area 2 or 3. Pruitt cannot be in area 1, so Pruitt must be in area 2 or 3. That leaves Jefferson as the only ranger who can be in area 1.

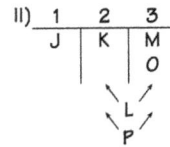

II)
```
   1   2   3
   J   K   M
           O
         \ L /
           P
```

Jefferson must be in area 1, eliminating **(A)** and **(B)**. Larson must be in area 2 or 3, eliminating **(C)**. Olsen is in area 3, eliminating **(D)**. That leaves **(E)** as the correct answer. Pruitt can certainly be assigned to area 3.

11. (B) "If" / Could Be True

For this question, Larson and Olsen are assigned to the same area. Larson also has to be assigned to an area with Koguchi or Mendez. That would put three rangers in one area, which is the maximum. If they were assigned to area 3, the third ranger would be Mendez (Rule 1). If they were assigned to area 1 or 2, the third ranger would have to be Koguchi. However, Olsen cannot be assigned to area 1 (Rule 2), and if Olsen were in area 2, Jefferson would have to be added to the group with Koguchi (Rule 4), which would put four rangers in one area. Thus, it would have to be Larson, Mendez, and Olsen together in area 3, with nobody else.

Pruitt cannot be assigned to area 1, so Pruitt will go in area 2. With Olsen in area 3, Jefferson and Koguchi would have to be split between areas 1 and 2 (Rule 4).

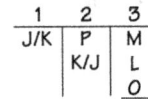

```
    1    2    3
   J/K   P    M
        K/J   L
              O
```

Larson and Olsen are in area 3, so that eliminates **(C)** and **(D)**. With Mendez in area 3, there's no room for Jefferson or Pruitt in area 3, which eliminates **(A)** and **(E)**. However, Koguchi could still be assigned to area 2, making **(B)** the correct answer.

This question can also be answered quickly with the Limited Options. If Larson and Olsen are together, that can only happen in Option II (because Olsen is established in area 2, and Larson can only go to areas 1 or 3 in the Option I sketch). So, using the Option II sketch, Larson gets added to area 3 as the third and final ranger. That forces Pruitt to area 2 and leaves Jefferson and Koguchi. One will have to go to area 1 and the other to area 2 so that they stay separated (Rule 4). That also leads to **(B)**.

12. (A) "If" / Must Be True

For this question, Jefferson is assigned to area 2. In that case, Olsen cannot also be assigned to area 2. Otherwise, Jefferson would be with Koguchi, too (Rule 4). However, that would leave nobody for area 1 because Pruitt cannot be in area 1 (Rule 1), and Larson cannot be alone (Rule 3). This was seen as impossible in Option I, so this question must be asking about Option II in which Olsen must be in area 3.

```
  1   2   3
 ┌───┬───┐
 │ J │ M │
 │   │ O │
```

That leaves Koguchi, Larson, and Pruitt. With Olsen in area 3, Jefferson and Koguchi must be split up (Rule 4). Koguchi could not be with Mendez in area 3 without violating Rule 3. Therefore, Koguchi must be assigned to area 1.

```
  1   2   3
 ┌───┬───┐
 │ K │ J │ M │
 │   │   │ O │
```

That makes **(A)** the correct answer. The remaining answers are all possible, but need not be true, except for **(C)**, which must be false.

Game 3: Economics TAs

Step 1: Overview

Situation: Teaching assistants being assigned to courses in an economics department

Entities: Six assistants (Ramos, Smith, Taj, Vogel, Yi, Zane) and three courses (Labor, Markets, Pricing)

Action: Distribution. Determine the course to which each assistant is assigned.

Limitations: Each assistant will be assigned to exactly one course, and each course will have at least one assistant.

Step 2: Sketch

List the assistants by initial and set up a chart with three columns, one for each course. Because each course gets at least one assistant, add one space to each area. The remaining spaces will be filled in as the game proceeds.

```
        R S T V Y Z
       Lab  Mar  Pri
       ───  ───  ───
```

Step 3: Rules

Rule 1 sets a numeric limitation to Markets. There will be exactly two assistants assigned to that course. Add a second slot to the Markets column, and close the column off.

Rule 2 creates a block, with Smith and Taj together. They could be assigned to any of the courses so far, and other assistants can be assigned with them. Draw this block off to the side.

```
┌───┐
│ S │
│ T │
└───┘
```

Rule 3 dictates that Vogel and Yi be assigned to different courses. Draw a note of this to the side.

```
┌───┐
│ V │
│╱Y │
└───┘
```

Rule 4 provides some Formal Logic. If either Yi or Zane is assigned to Pricing, they both are. By contrapositive, if they're not both in Pricing, then neither of them is. Essentially, this sets up two possible outcomes: either Yi and Zane are both in Pricing, or neither of them are. You can draw this rule off to the side or set up Limited Options.

Step 4: Deductions

By Rule 4, there are two options. In the first option, Yi and Zane are both assigned to Pricing. In the second option, neither of them is assigned to Pricing.

The first option would establish five spaces: one in Labor, two in Markets, and two in Pricing. That leaves one more space, which could go in Labor or Pricing. With Yi in Pricing, Vogel cannot be assigned to Pricing (Rule 3). Also, there's only room for one more assistant in Pricing, at most, so Smith and Taj

cannot be assigned to Pricing. That means only Ramos could, but need not be. Ramos could still be in either of the remaining courses.

```
I)  Lab  Mar  Pri
    ───  ─┬─  ─Y─
        │  │   Z
    ────┴──┴──────
         ~S,~T,~V
```

In the second option, Yi and Zane will not be assigned to Pricing, but they could be assigned to either of the other courses. Note that they could be assigned together, but need not be. It is possible that one is assigned to Labor while the other is assigned to Markets. Unfortunately, that's as much as can be deduced, as the one block of entities (Smith and Taj) could still be assigned to any of the three courses.

```
II)  Lab  Mar  Pri
     ───  ─┬─  ───
         │  │
     ────┴──┴──────
          ~Y,~Z
```

Step 5: Questions

13. (A) Partial Acceptability

The correct answer to this question will be a possible assignment for the Pricing course. As with regular Acceptability questions, start by testing the rules one at a time to see which answers violate those rules. If any answers remain, test them by considering the unlisted entities to find the one answer that is possible.

Rule 1 cannot be directly tested because the answers only list the Pricing assignments. **(D)** violates Rule 2 by assigning Taj to the course without Smith. **(E)** violates Rule 3 by assigning Vogel and Yi together. **(B)** violates Rule 4 by assigning Yi to Pricing without Zane. That leaves **(A)** and **(C)**.

As determined in setting up the first option, Smith and Taj could not be assigned with Yi and Zane. That would leave just two assistants for the remaining courses. However, Labor needs at least one and Marketing needs two (Rule 1). There wouldn't be enough assistants. That eliminates **(C)**, leaving **(A)** as the correct answer.

14. (B) Partial Acceptability (CANNOT)

The correct answer will be an assignment for Labor that cannot happen. That means the remaining four answers will list assignments that *are* possible for Labor.

Note that each answer choice lists exactly two assistants, meaning that for each answer, there will be two assistants in Labor. There must be two assistants in Markets (Rule 1). That leaves Pricing for the final two assistants.

One department must get Smith and Taj together. Of the remaining four assistants, Vogel and Yi cannot be together.

So, they will be split between the remaining courses, resulting in the remaining assistants—Ramos and Zane—being split to pair up with Vogel and Yi.

Lab	Mar	Pri
—	—	—
S	V	Y
T	R/Z	Z/R

With Ramos and Zane split up, it is impossible for them to be the sole assistants in Labor. That makes **(B)** the correct answer. Any of the remaining pairs are possible assignments to Labor.

15. (A) Could Be True

The correct answer for this question will be the only one that presents a possible outcome. The remaining answers will all be false, i.e., impossible.

If Ramos and Vogel are assigned to Markets, Smith and Taj could be assigned to Labor, and Yi and Zane could be assigned to Pricing (or vice versa).

Lab	Mar	Pri		Lab	Mar	Pri
S	R	Y	or	Y	R	S
T	V	Z		Z	V	T

This is certainly possible, making **(A)** the correct answer. For the record:

If Ramos was in Markets with Taj, Smith would have to be with them (Rule 2). Similarly, if Smith was in Markets with Vogel, Taj would have to be with them. However, only two assistants can be assigned to Markets (Rule 1). That eliminates **(B)** and **(C)**.

If Smith and Zane were assigned to Pricing, then Taj (Rule 2) and Yi (Rule 4) would be also. However, that would not leave enough assistants to fill the space in Labor and the two spaces in Markets. Therefore, that eliminates **(D)**.

Additionally, if Zane is assigned to Pricing, so is Yi, which means Vogel couldn't be there (Rule 3). That eliminates **(E)**.

16. (C) "If" / Must Be False (CANNOT Be True)

For this question, Vogel is assigned to the same course as Zane. By Rule 3, Vogel and Yi cannot be together, so Yi and Zane will not be together. If Yi and Zane cannot be together, neither of them will be in Pricing (Rule 4). Thus, one must be assigned to Labor and the other to Markets. It helps to draw both possibilities.

In the first outcome, Yi is assigned to Labor, and Zane (with Vogel) is assigned to Markets. In that case, Markets is filled up. Smith and Taj could be assigned to Labor or Pricing, as could Ramos.

Lab	Mar	Pri
Y	Z	
	V	
↑		R
S		
T		

In the second outcome, Yi is assigned to Markets, and Zane (with Vogel) is assigned to Labor. With only one position left in Markets, there's not enough room for Smith and Taj. So, that position will be filled by Ramos, leaving Smith and Taj to be assigned to Pricing.

Lab	Mar	Pri
Z	Y	S
V	R	T

Neither outcome allows for Taj to be assigned to Markets. That makes **(C)** the correct answer. All of the remaining answers are possible in at least one option.

17. (D) "If" / Must Be True

For this question, Ramos will be assigned to one course with no other assistant. Markets requires two assistants, so Ramos could only do Labor or Pricing alone. Test both outcomes.

In the first outcome, Ramos is the only assistant assigned to Labor. Vogel and Yi must be split between Markets and Pricing (Rule 3). That leaves only one space in Markets. That's not enough for both Smith and Taj, so they must be assigned to Pricing, meaning Zane must take up the last space in Markets.

Lab	Mar	Pri
R	V/Y	Y/V
	Z	S
		T

Yi cannot be in Pricing without Zane (Rule 4), so Yi will be assigned to Markets, leaving Vogel to be assigned to Pricing.

Lab	Mar	Pri
R	Y	V
	Z	S
		T

In the second outcome, Ramos is the only assistant assigned to Pricing. Again, Vogel and Yi must be split, this time between Labor and Markets. With only one space remaining in Markets, Smith and Taj must be assigned to Labor. That leaves Zane for the final space in Markets. In this case, Vogel and Yi cannot be assigned with certainty. One will be assigned to Labor. The other will be assigned to Markets.

Lab	Mar	Pri
V/Y	Y/V	R
S	Z	
T		

In both cases, Zane is assigned to Markets, making **(D)** the correct answer. The remaining answers are all possible, but need not be true.

Game 4: Computer Virus

Step 1: Overview

Situation: A computer virus infecting computers on a network

Entities: Six computers (P, Q, R, S, T, U)

Action: Strict Sequencing. Determine the order in which the computers were infected.

Limitations: Exactly one computer was infected from outside the network. Each computer received the virus exactly once and (except for the first computer) from one of the other computers in the network.

Step 2: Sketch

At first glance, this appears to be a standard Sequencing game. However, there's an unusual twist that may not be apparent until the first rule. When a computer is infected, it can pass the virus to more than one computer, essentially creating separate sequences. In that case, a series of slots will not be useful. Instead, it will ultimately be more important to see how the virus branches out from each computer and continues infecting computers in order. For instance, if P transmitted the virus to Q and R, that would create two separate branches. In that case, it would be most helpful to use arrows to indicate transmission from one computer to the next, like so:

$$P \underset{R}{\overset{Q}{<}}$$

Note that these arrows do not work like Loose Sequencing branches. Instead of indicating relative relationships, they show direct transmission from one computer to the next.

Unfortunately, there's no way of determining when in the sequence the branches will occur. So, just list the entities and head to the rules.

Step 3: Rules

Rule 1 creates a numeric restriction. Any computer that transmitted the virus could only do so to a maximum of two other computers. Make a note of this to the side (e.g., "Max. 2 comp. get virus from 1 comp.").

Rule 2 establishes that S transmitted the virus to just one other computer. Draw S with one arrow to a blank space, and make a note of the numeric restriction:

$$S \rightarrow \underline{\quad} \quad (exactly\ 1)$$

Note that the computer that received the virus from S could have passed it along to another computer. So, multiple computers could have received the virus after S, but only one got it *directly* from S.

Rule 3 indicates that there will be at least one computer that passes the virus to two other computers, and that computer

will infect R and S. Draw one space with two arrows leading to R and S.

$$\underline{\quad} \underset{S}{\overset{R}{<}}$$

Rule 4 states that computer R or T transmitted the virus to Q:

$$R/T \rightarrow Q$$

Rule 5 states that computer T or U transmitted the virus to P:

$$T/U \rightarrow P$$

Step 4: Deductions

Rules 2 and 3 can be combined because of the Duplicated entity S. By Rule 3, there is a computer that transmitted the virus to S (as well as R), and then S passed the virus along to yet another computer (Rule 2). That creates a string of four computers:

$$\underline{\quad} \underset{S \rightarrow \underline{\quad}}{\overset{R}{<}}$$

The computer that passed the virus to both R and S could be any of the remaining computers. However, S did not transmit the virus to Q (Rule 4) or P (Rule 5). That means it must have transmitted the virus to either T or U (but not both because Rule 2 says "exactly one").

The final point to consider is which computer could have been infected first (i.e., from outside the network). By the last three rules, P, Q, R, and S were all infected by another computer within the network. That means only T or U could have been the first computer infected. Note that these are the same two computers that could have received the virus from S. Therefore, between T and U, one of them will be the first computer infected, and one of them will get the virus from S.

$$\underset{1st}{\overset{T/U}{\underline{\quad}}} \quad \underline{\quad} \underset{S \rightarrow U/T}{\overset{R}{<}}$$

Step 5: Questions

18. (D) Partial Acceptability

The correct answer will list a possible order of infection from the first computer infected to Q. The answers are only partial because they only list the direct route to Q, leaving out any separate branches to other computers. As with any other Acceptability question, start by going through the rules one at a time, eliminating answers that violate those rules. Then, if needed, fill in information for any remaining answers to find the only one that is possible.

Because each answer shows transmission from one computer to just one other computer, none of them will violate Rule 1. Similarly, the two answers that list S show transmission to just one other computer, so no answer violates Rule 2. By

Rule 3, there must have been a computer that transmitted the virus to R, so R could not be the first computer infected. That eliminates **(A)**. Also by Rule 3, the same computer transmitted the virus to R and S. That eliminates **(B)**, which has T transmit the virus to S, but S transmits the virus to R. **(C)** violates Rule 4 because Q could not get the virus from U. Neither remaining answer violates Rule 5, as they both have T or U transmit the virus to P.

(D) lists transmission from U to P to R to Q. By Rule 3, P would also have transmitted the virus to S. By Rule 2, S would transmit the virus to one other computer. T is left, so that is acceptable.

$$U \rightarrow P \begin{array}{c} \nearrow R \rightarrow Q \\ \searrow S \rightarrow T \end{array}$$

(E) lists transmission from U to T to P to R to Q. Again, by Rule 3, P would have also transmitted the virus to S. However, by Rule 2, S had to transmit the virus to another computer, but there are no computers left.

$$U \rightarrow T \rightarrow P \begin{array}{c} \nearrow R \rightarrow Q \\ \searrow S \rightarrow ? \end{array}$$

Therefore, **(E)** is impossible, leaving **(D)** as the correct answer.

19. (E) Could Be True

The correct answer to this question will be a computer that could have been infected from outside the network. The remaining answers will list computers that could not, i.e., they must have been infected from *inside* the network.

R and S were infected from another computer inside the network (Rule 3), as were Q (Rule 4) and P (Rule 5). That leaves only T and U, either of which could have been infected from outside the network. That makes **(E)** the correct answer.

20. (A) "If" / Must Be True

For this question, T did not transmit the virus to any other computer. By Rule 4, that means R transmitted the virus to Q. And by Rule 5, U must have transmitted the virus to P.

One computer transmitted the virus to both R and S (Rule 3). It cannot be Q, which received the virus *from* R in this case. It cannot be T, which did not transmit the virus at all in this case. And it cannot be U, which already transmitted the virus to P in this case and cannot transmit it to another two computers (Rule 1). That means P must have transmitted the virus to R and S. So, the virus went from U to P, from P to R and S, and from R to Q. It still needs to be transmitted from S to one other computer (Rule 2), and only T is left.

$$U \rightarrow P \begin{array}{c} \nearrow R \rightarrow Q \\ \searrow S \rightarrow T \end{array}$$

With that, **(A)** must be true and is the correct answer.

21. (C) Could Be True EXCEPT

Four answers will list computers that could have transmitted the virus to two other computers. The correct answer will be a computer that could not, i.e., a computer that could have only transmitted the virus to one other computer at most.

By Rule 2, S can only transmit the virus to one other computer, but S is not listed in the answers. P is said to transmit the virus to two computers in the last question of the game (and it also did so in the previous question). That eliminates **(A)**.

There must be a computer that transmits the virus to both R and S. That could be any of the remaining computers (P, Q, T, and U), which leaves R as the only possible answer of which computer *cannot* transfer the virus to two computers. Thus, **(C)** is the correct answer.

To confirm that R can't transmit the virus to two computers, consider which computers R *could* transmit the virus to. R can certainly transmit the virus to Q (Rule 4). However, R cannot transmit the virus to P (Rule 5) or S (Rule 3). Because of the last three rules, T or U has to be infected from outside the network (i.e., T or U must be the first computer in the sequence), and S has to transmit the virus to a computer, which cannot be P (Rule 5), Q (Rule 4), or R (Rule 3). So, S has to transmit the virus to T or U, whichever one was not infected first. That means Q is the *only* computer R can infect, confirming **(C)** as the correct answer.

22. (C) Completely Determine

The correct answer will be a piece of information that, if true, would allow the entire order of virus transmission to be determined with no uncertainty. The correct answer would have to help determine which computer was infected first, the one computer that transmitted the virus to both R and S, and the one computer infected by computer S.

If R transmitted the virus to Q, either T or U could still be the first computer infected with S infecting the other. With more than one possible outcome, **(A)** is eliminated.

If T transmitted the virus to Q, T could still be the first computer infected, but so could U. There's more than one outcome possible, so **(B)** is eliminated.

If T transmitted the virus to S, then it also transmitted the virus to R (Rule 3). Having transmitted the virus to two other computers, it could not transmit the virus to any others. That means R transmitted the virus to Q (Rule 4) and U transmitted the virus to P (Rule 5). S had to transmit to one other computer (Rule 2), and only computer U is left.

$$T \begin{array}{c} \nearrow R \rightarrow Q \\ \searrow S \rightarrow U \rightarrow P \end{array}$$

That indicates every transmission, making **(C)** the correct answer. For the record:

If U transmitted the virus to P, then U could still be the first computer infected, but so could T. There's more than one outcome possible, so **(D)** is eliminated.

If U transmitted the virus to R, then U also transmitted the virus to S (Rule 3). Having transmitted the virus to two other computers, it could not transmit the virus to any other. That means T transmitted the virus to P (Rule 5). S must transmit the virus to exactly one computer (Rule 2), but it can't be Q (Rule 4), so the only computer left that's possible for S to transmit the virus to is T. However, it is still unknown which of T or R transmitted the virus to Q (Rule 4).

$$U < \genfrac{}{}{0pt}{}{R \quad Q?}{S \rightarrow T \rightarrow P}$$

With more than one possible outcome, **(E)** is eliminated.

23. (C) "If" / Must Be True

For this question, P transmits the virus to two other computers, and it is the only computer to do so. One computer has to transmit a virus to both R and S, so it must be P in this case. Either T or U will transmit the virus to P (Rule 5). S cannot transmit the virus to Q (Rule 4), but it must transmit the virus to one other computer. Only T or U are left.

$$T/U \rightarrow P < \genfrac{}{}{0pt}{}{R \quad Q?}{S \rightarrow U/T}$$

That leaves Q, which received the virus from R or T (Rule 4). Either way, all of the other computers are accounted for, so Q would not have transmitted the virus to any other computer. That makes **(C)** the correct answer. All of the remaining answers are possible, but need not be true. They could all be false, depending on whether T or U was infected first and whether R or T transmitted the virus to Q.

Section IV: Logical Reasoning

Q#	Question Type	Correct	Difficulty
1	Paradox	D	★
2	Assumption (Necessary)	A	★
3	Paradox	D	★
4	Assumption (Sufficient)	A	★★
5	Flaw	D	★★
6	Assumption (Necessary)	B	★★
7	Principle (Identify/Strengthen)	D	★
8	Assumption (Necessary)	B	★
9	Flaw	A	★★
10	Assumption (Sufficient)	A	★
11	Main Point	E	★★
12	Method of Argument	E	★★★★
13	Principle (Parallel)	C	★
14	Strengthen	D	★
15	Principle (Identify/Strengthen)	A	★
16	Parallel Flaw	D	★
17	Main Point	A	★
18	Flaw	B	★
19	Weaken	B	★★★
20	Point at Issue	B	★★
21	Assumption (Necessary)	C	★★★★
22	Strengthen	C	★★★★
23	Inference	B	★★
24	Role of a Statement	B	★★★★
25	Inference	C	★★★

1. (D) Paradox

Step 1: Identify the Question Type

The question asks for something that "helps to resolve the apparent discrepancy," making this a Paradox question.

Step 2: Untangle the Stimulus

In cold-blooded animals, cool weather weakens muscle power. The veiled chameleon is a cold-blooded animal, so its tongue naturally takes longer to retract when it gets cooler. However, it doesn't take much longer for the tongue to extend.

Step 3: Make a Prediction

The correct answer will answer the central mystery: why does it take longer for the tongue to retract, but not to extend? The solution is hinted at in the first sentence; cooler weather affects "muscle power." So, if retraction requires muscle power but extension does not, then that would resolve the issue.

Step 4: Evaluate the Answer Choices

(D) resolves the issue. Cool weather weakens muscle power. So, if retraction is powered by muscles, retraction would be slower in cool weather. Additionally, with extension driven by energy, not muscle power, there's no reason to expect a slowdown.

(A) is an Irrelevant Comparison. What is true for most cold-blooded animals has no bearing on why the chameleon's tongue only slows down during retraction.

(B) is Out of Scope. The distance the tongue can extend does nothing to explain why it doesn't slow down in cool weather.

(C) is also Out of Scope. Where the chameleon lives does nothing to explain why tongue extension does not slow down much in cool weather.

(E) is an Irrelevant Comparison. The mystery is not about chameleons versus other animals. The mystery is about why retraction slows down but extension does not. This offers no information about extension, so the mystery goes unsolved.

2. (A) Assumption (Necessary)

Step 1: Identify the Question Type

The question asks for an assumption that the argument *requires*, making this a Necessary Assumption question.

Step 2: Untangle the Stimulus

The author concludes (*so*) that Acme will have to declare bankruptcy. This is based on some Formal Logic rules. If Acme's annual earnings fall below $1 million, it must repay its bank loan in full, in which case it will go bankrupt.

If	earnings below $1M	→	repay bank loan in full	→	bankruptcy

Unfortunately, Acme overstated its earnings in the previous year.

Step 3: Make a Prediction

By the Formal Logic, Acme would have to declare bankruptcy if it's earnings one year dipped below $1 million. The evidence only claims that Acme overstated its earnings for one year. However, it's possible that it originally reported $2 million dollars but only earned $1.5 million. In that case, it overstated its earnings but still didn't have to declare bankruptcy. The only way the author can logically conclude Acme has to declare bankruptcy is if the earnings were actually below $1 million. That's what the author is assuming happened.

Step 4: Evaluate the Answer Choices

(A) is correct. If Acme earned *more* than $1 million last year, then the author's evidence about overstatement is irrelevant and the argument is invalid. The author must assume that the actual earnings were *less* than $1 million.

(B) is Out of Scope. The bank loan by itself is enough to cause the threat of bankruptcy. The author need not assume anything about other debts.

(C) is irrelevant. It doesn't matter how many years involved overstatement. Bankruptcy would be required even if just one year's earnings fall below $1 million.

(D) is irrelevant. The author's conclusion is based on last year's earnings, not this year's earnings. While dropping below $1 million this year would certainly confirm the author's conclusion, it's not necessary. As long as *last* year's earnings were below $1 million, the author still has a valid argument, regardless of what happens this year.

(E) is irrelevant. It's a pleasant thought, but there's no need for hypothetical situations here. The fact is that Acme *does* have to repay the loan if earnings drop below $1 million. No amount of "what ifs" are going to change that.

3. (D) Paradox

Step 1: Identify the Question Type

The correct answer will "resolve the apparent conflict," making this a Paradox question.

Step 2: Untangle the Stimulus

Hospital patients in private rooms tend to get fewer infections and are released sooner than those in semiprivate rooms. However, patients at Woodville's hospital are all placed in semiprivate rooms, but they're not any worse off than similar patients in private rooms in nearby hospitals.

Step 3: Make a Prediction

The correct answer will address the central mystery: why are patients in semiprivate rooms at Woodville's hospital having the same experience as patients in private rooms at other hospitals? The patients are said to be similar, so it's not as if Woodville's hospital just happens to get easier patients. There must be something else about Woodville's hospital that benefits its patients. It's not worth predicting an exact solution. Just know that the correct answer will indicate something distinct about Woodville's hospital that helps make its semiprivate rooms equivalent to other hospitals' private rooms.

Step 4: Evaluate the Answer Choices

(D) resolves the issue. The rooms may technically be semiprivate, but placing only one person per room effectively creates a private environment. So, patients would still get the benefit of a private room, even though the room could, in theory, house multiple patients.

(A) does not help. Even if the doctors are all the same, the rooms at Woodville are still only semiprivate, which should still result in more problems.

(B) is Out of Scope. The age of the building has nothing to do with a patient's infection rate or length of stay. At worst, one could argue (perhaps unfairly) that Woodville's hospital being 40 years older might make it out-of-date. Nevertheless, that would just make it *more* unusual that patients are doing just as well.

(C) is a 180. This is exactly what should make semiprivate rooms more problematic—and yet patients in semiprivate rooms at Woodville's hospital are *still* doing just as well as patients in private rooms.

(E) is Out of Scope. The location of the hospital should have no effect on how people recover once they're in the hospital.

4. (A) Assumption (Sufficient)

Step 1: Identify the Question Type

The correct answer will be something that, *if* assumed, would make the argument valid. That makes this a Sufficient Assumption question.

Step 2: Untangle the Stimulus

The economist predicts that unemployment will soon decrease. The evidence is based on two possible scenarios: 1) If government spending significantly increases, the economy is stimulated and unemployment will decrease. 2) If government spending significantly decreases, businesses keep more earnings and hire more workers, so unemployment will decrease.

Step 3: Make a Prediction

Accepting the economist's logic, either of the two scenarios presented would indeed reduce unemployment. However, what if spending stays constant? What if the change in spending is not significant? Those scenarios are not accounted for. The economist's entire argument rests on the assumption that spending will indeed increase or decrease significantly.

Step 4: Evaluate the Answer Choices

(A) is correct. If government spending significantly increases or decreases next year, then either case would set off the economist's logic and confirm the prediction that unemployment will decrease.

(B) is irrelevant. Policies that are *intended* to reduce unemployment won't necessarily work. Besides, the economist's argument is based on government spending, not new policies.

(C) is not good enough. This ensures a decrease in unemployment under one condition: demand for workers increases. However, there's no way to know if that condition will be met, so this cannot confirm the economist's prediction.

(D) is Out of Scope. What will happen to the economy in the long run does nothing to confirm the economist's prediction about unemployment in the near future.

(E) is a 180. This offers a situation in which unemployment will *not* decrease, which would go against the economist's prediction. **(E)** creates two improper contrapositives of the Formal Logic chains in the evidence, negating but not reversing the terms. Those improper contrapositives would not guarantee the economist's conclusion.

5. (D) Flaw

Step 1: Identify the Question Type

Tyne is said to have *misinterpreted* something, which means she has committed a logical flaw. The correct answer will identify a word in Marisa's argument that Tyne's argument uses or addresses improperly.

Step 2: Untangle the Stimulus

Marisa argues for the need to loosen zoning regulations. The current regulations are restricting development, which leads to reduced property values. Tyne disagrees, arguing that regulations are indeed restricting development but that they're actually preserving the value of natural, undisturbed lands.

Step 3: Make a Prediction

Marisa and Tyne agree that regulations restrict development. However, Marisa is complaining about the effect on property values. Tyne brings up the "value of natural, undisturbed lands." They both use the word *value*, but Tyne completely addresses the wrong type of value. Marisa doesn't care about environmental value; she cares about money. It's that word *value* that Tyne misinterprets.

Step 4: Evaluate the Answer Choices

(D) is correct. Marisa is talking about the financial value of property, while Tyne addresses the environmental value of undisturbed land.

(A) is a 180. Marisa and Tyne are both talking about the same regulations, so there's no misinterpretation there.

(B) is a 180. Both speakers use development in the same sense: the construction of buildings on unused land.

(C) is a 180. Marisa uses *prohibitive* to mean "restrictive." Tyne's argument is consistent with that definition.

(E) is a Distortion. It's not the significance of the value that Tyne misinterprets. It's the type of value itself.

6. (B) Assumption (Necessary)

Step 1: Identify the Question Type

The question asks for something the argument "requires assuming," making this a Necessary Assumption question.

Step 2: Untangle the Stimulus

The scientist is arguing that results of animal research can be skewed. The evidence is that research animals get plenty of food but exercise very little, and studies depend on the assumption that animals are healthy (as illustrated by a pointless example).

Step 3: Make a Prediction

The results would be skewed if the assumption is wrong, i.e., the research animals are not actually healthy. However, the scientist only cites the existence of "ample food" and "little exercise." The scientist must be assuming that ample food and little exercise are actually unhealthy for the animals.

Step 4: Evaluate the Answer Choices

(B) is correct, making the necessary link between the ample food/little exercise environment and the animals' health.

(A) is a Distortion. Even if animals are healthy in a better environment, that doesn't mean the current environment is *unhealthy*, as the scientist assumes.

(C) is a 180. If access to ample food and little exercise is normal, then there's no reason to believe laboratories are artificially creating an unhealthy environment for the animals.

(D) is irrelevant. Even if some studies do take living conditions into account, that still has no effect on the scientist's argument, which is about studies that *don't*. It's *those* studies that the scientist is criticizing.

(E) is a 180. This suggests that the ample food does not necessarily lead to overeating. Animals will continue to eat the same amount. That contradicts the scientist's assumption that ample food would lead to an unhealthy environment.

7. (D) Principle (Identify/Strengthen)

Step 1: Identify the Question Type

The correct answer will be a principle that will be used to *justify* the argument given, making this an Identify the Principle question that mimics a Strengthen question.

Step 2: Untangle the Stimulus

The negotiator concludes ([*therefore*]) that countries should not adopt trade policies that hinder other countries' prosperity. The evidence is that prosperity brings about political freedom.

Step 3: Make a Prediction

The conclusion is about prosperity, but the evidence suggests that the negotiator's ultimate concern is political freedom. So, the negotiator is suggesting that trade policies should not prevent political freedom in other countries. The correct answer will be a general rule that validates the negotiator's desire to protect political freedom.

Step 4: Evaluate the Answer Choices

(D) validates the negotiator's recommendation to avoid hindering prosperity, as that in turn would hinder political freedom.

(A) is a Distortion. The negotiator is not recommending policies that *encourage* freedom. The negotiator is recommending *against* policies that *hinder* freedom.

(B) brings up overall well-being, which has no bearing on the negotiator's argument.

(C) is Extreme and a Distortion. Political freedom does not have to be the *primary* motivator for seeking prosperity. Besides, this provides no justification for the negotiator's recommendation to avoid certain policies.

(E) is a Distortion. The negotiator's argument is about preventing issues in any *other* country, not necessarily problems within the negotiator's country itself.

8. (B) Assumption (Necessary)

Step 1: Identify the Question Type

The correct answer will be an "assumption required by the argument," making this a Necessary Assumption question.

Step 2: Untangle the Stimulus

The author concludes ([*thus*]) that great works of art are rare. The evidence is that a combination of tremendous skill and extraordinary creativity is both necessary and sufficient for great art.

Step 3: Make a Prediction

If it takes high levels of skill and creativity to create great art, but that great art is rare, the author must assume that that combination of high skill and creativity is also rare.

Step 4: Evaluate the Answer Choices

(B) is correct. The combination of creativity and skill must be rare to claim that great art is rare. If that combination were common, then great art would also be common (as the author states that "the resulting product [of combining skill and creativity] is a great work of art").

(A) is irrelevant. Even if some artists have less-than-stellar skills, there could still be plenty of other artists who are highly skilled and capable of creating lots of great art.

(C) is a Faulty Use of Detail. This essentially repeats the first sentence of the stimulus. However, if there are enough such artists, then the author has no reason to claim that great art would be rare. So, **(C)** does nothing to fill in the gap between the evidence and conclusion.

(D) is irrelevant. The argument is not about the rarity of great *artists*, but the rarity of great *art*. Even if highly skilled and creative artists are rare, they could be prolific enough to create tons of great art.

(E) is not necessary. Even if the most skilled and creative artists create just a few great artworks, there could still be lots of such artists, which would mean plenty of great art.

9. (A) Flaw

Step 1: Identify the Question Type

The correct answer will describe why the argument is *flawed*, making this a Flaw question.

Step 2: Untangle the Stimulus

The advertisement concludes ([*s*]*o*) that eating Fantastic Flakes every morning will help you become physically fit. The evidence is that people who eat cereal tend to exercise more than people who don't eat cereal, and exercise helps you become fit.

Step 3: Make a Prediction

The evidence never directly indicates that cereal itself makes you fit. Exercise does that. People who exercise just *tend* to eat more cereal. The advertisement is thus implying that the cereal *makes* people exercise, which in turn leads to being physically fit. This is a classic case of correlation versus causation. People who exercise tend to eat cereal, but that doesn't mean cereal is the *cause* of them exercising. The correct answer will address this commonly tested flaw.

Step 4: Evaluate the Answer Choices

(A) is correct, describing the implication of causality (cereal makes you exercise more) based on a mere correlation (people who exercise happen to eat more cereal).

(B) is an Irrelevant Comparison. The advertisement is not pushing nutrition. It's only pushing the cereal's influence on exercise and thus its influence on becoming physically fit.

(C) is Extreme. Nothing is stated or implied to be the *sole* predictor of anything. The advertisement argues that the cereal will make you fit, but it never suggests it's the only way to become fit.

(D) brings up the flaw of representativeness. However, there's no sample group in the evidence. All of the evidence is about what's true for people in general.

(E) brings up the flaw of applying a group trait to individual members. However, there is no characteristic applied to any group, and the conclusion does not apply a characteristic to individual members of any group.

10. (A) Assumption (Sufficient)

Step 1: Identify the Question Type

The question asks for something that, *if* assumed, allows the conclusion to be drawn. That makes this a Sufficient Assumption question.

Step 2: Untangle the Stimulus

The journalist concludes ([*s*]*o*) that the critics are mistaken. They claim entertainment decreases the caliber of news reporting, which means the journalist is arguing that entertainment does *not* decrease the caliber. The evidence is that the greatest journalists have been the most entertaining.

Step 3: Make a Prediction

The evidence is about the "greatest journalists," but the conclusion is about the "caliber of the reporting" itself. The journalist simply assumes that the greatest journalists provided high-caliber reporting.

Step 4: Evaluate the Answer Choices

(A) is correct, making the connection between the greatest journalists and the caliber of their reporting.

(B) is not good enough. Even if the greatest journalists have been entertainers, that still does not speak to the caliber of the reporting itself.

(C) is not good enough. This just connects greatness to value "in some sense." If that sense does not involve the caliber of the reporting, then it's irrelevant to the argument at hand.

(D) is something the journalist might agree with, but it offers no support for the conclusion about the caliber of the reporting.

(E) is a 180 at worst. This suggests that entertainment *can* be bad for news reporting, which contradicts the journalist's reasoning.

11. (E) Main Point

Step 1: Identify the Question Type

The correct answer will be the "overall conclusion," or main point, of the argument.

Step 2: Untangle the Stimulus

The linguist starts out with a fact: three out of four subfamilies of Austronesian languages are spoken only in Taiwan, while the fourth is spoken elsewhere. *Since* indicates a piece of evidence: all four subfamilies are based on the same language, which must have originated in one area. That leads the linguist to claim that Taiwan is that source country. *Hence*, the linguist reaches the final conclusion: Austronesian-speaking people originated in Taiwan and later migrated.

Step 3: Make a Prediction

The linguist starts off with a fact. After that, the rest of the argument starts with a single piece of evidence that leads to one conclusion after the other. However, each conclusion is just a subsidiary conclusion that acts as evidence for the next one until the linguist reaches the final point (*hence*). That final conclusion, that Austronesian-speaking people originated in Taiwan and then migrated, is the overall conclusion, ultimately supported by everything else before it.

Step 4: Evaluate the Answer Choices

(E) correctly states, practically word for word from the stimulus, the overall conclusion.

(A) is merely a fact presented at the beginning. It is background information and nothing more.

(B) is too vague. This is more a principle or an assumption behind the linguist's argument. However, it does not adequately express the more specific conclusion drawn that Taiwan is the likely origin of the Austronesian-speaking peoples.

(C) is certainly *a* conclusion backed up by the facts in the argument. However, it is merely a subsidiary conclusion, one that is ultimately used as evidence to support the overall conclusion about where the *people* originated.

(D) is more a principle or assumption behind the linguist's argument. The overall conclusion actually specifies the location (Taiwan), rather than presents an open-ended concept.

12. (E) Method of Argument

Step 1: Identify the Question Type

The word *by* indicates a Method of Argument question. In essence, the question is asking, "By what method does Young respond to West?" The correct answer will describe *how* Young responds rather than *what* Young says.

Step 2: Untangle the Stimulus

West argues that Haynes is the worst of the company's three quality control inspectors. The evidence is that half of the defective appliances returned last year were inspected by

Haynes. Young counters that Haynes is responsible for inspecting the vast majority of appliances.

Step 3: Make a Prediction

West's argument would be valid if every inspector inspected roughly the same number of appliances. In that case, one would expect each inspector to be responsible for an average of one-third of the defective returns. Haynes being responsible for *half* would surely look bad. However, Young's statement counters the assumption that all inspectors are performing the same amount of work. If Haynes is responsible for most appliances to begin with, then Haynes is not as bad as West suggests. The correct answer will point out Young's countering of West's assumption.

Step 4: Evaluate the Answer Choices

(E) correctly describes Young's denial of West's presupposition (i.e., assumption) that all inspectors are inspecting roughly an equal number of appliances.

(A) is inaccurate. West's negative conclusion about Haynes is based on statistics, not on some predetermined agenda against Haynes, and Young makes no suggestion otherwise.

(B) is a Distortion. Young merely questions the validity of West's conclusion, not its relevance.

(C) is a Distortion. West's premise that half of the returned appliances with defects were inspected by Haynes is *not* disputed by Young. Instead, Young disputes an *unstated* assumption. West never states how many appliances Haynes inspects, and so Young disputes West's interpretation of the data, not the data itself.

(D) is a Distortion. This suggests that Young is saying, "Haynes is pretty bad, but he's not the *worst.*" That's not Young's point at all.

13. (C) Principle (Parallel)

Step 1: Identify the Question Type

The correct answer will be a specific situation that "conforms most closely" to a principle. However, that principle is not directly provided. It is *illustrated* by the specific situation in the stimulus. Therefore, this is a relatively rare instance of a Parallel Principle question, which involves first identifying the principle, then applying it to the correct answer.

Step 2: Untangle the Stimulus

The author concludes that John, and not Emma, should be punished for breaking the window. The evidence is that, even though they both were playing with no regard to potential danger, it was ultimately John's action that broke the window.

Step 3: Make a Prediction

The author's judgment is based on who caused the accident directly, despite the fact that both players were acting improperly. The correct answer will apply the very same principle to an entirely different scenario: even if two people are doing something dangerous, only the one who directly causes an accident should be punished for it.

Step 4: Evaluate the Answer Choices

(C) applies the same principle. Even though two people (Terry and Chris) were acting dangerously, only the one who directly caused the accident (Chris) should be punished for it.

(A) does not match because only one person is involved, and nothing bad actually happened.

(B) does not match. The furniture didn't fit, so neither Linda nor Seung was directly responsible. Moreover, this does not apply punishment to one person over the other.

(D) does not match. In this case, neither Alexis nor Juan was responsible for the problem. Furthermore, this suggests that the owner should pay even though somebody *else* (the previous renter) caused the problem.

(E) does not match. This does fit the idea that two people are breaking a rule, but there is no situation where one of the two people caused damage to someone else's property. So, there is no way of applying the principle of punishing the person who caused the problem. For one, it never directly suggests Susan is responsible for her ankle injury, and not allowing her to hold the pond owner responsible is not parallel to making her compensate the owner for the damage.

14. (D) Strengthen

Step 1: Identify the Question Type

The question directly asks for something that will strengthen the researchers' argument.

Step 2: Untangle the Stimulus

The researchers present a hypothesis that the sound of a parent singing to an infant is affected by that parent's emotions. The researchers conclude in the last sentence that this hypothesis is correct. The evidence is an experiment in which psychologists were asked to listen to recordings of parents singing. For the most part, the psychologists were able to correctly identify which ones involved parents singing to an infant, and which ones involved no infant.

Step 3: Make a Prediction

The experiment adequately shows that the voices are noticeably different depending on whether a baby was present or not. However, there's still no evidence that this change in voices was due to the parents' *emotions*. To strengthen this argument, there needs to be some evidence connecting the vocal change to emotions.

Step 4: Evaluate the Answer Choices

(D) strengthens the argument, making it more likely that the emotions were somewhat responsible for the vocal differences.

(A) is an Irrelevant Comparison. The hypothesis is not about whose children produce the strongest emotions. It's about whether those emotions affect the singing voice, regardless of whose children are involved or the intensity of the emotions.

(B) is a 180 at worst. This suggests that there were other factors involved, and perhaps the knowledge of being recorded played a role in vocal quality. In any case, it does nothing to connect vocal quality to one's emotions.

(C) confirms that emotions vary depending on whether or not an infant is present. However, it still does not strengthen the concept that those emotions are responsible for the change in vocal quality.

(E) is irrelevant. What people believe is not adequate evidence to support what actually happens.

15. (A) Principle (Identify/Strengthen)

Step 1: Identify the Question Type

The correct answer will be a principle that "helps to justify" the reasoning provided, making this an Identify the Principle question that mimics a Strengthen question.

Step 2: Untangle the Stimulus

There are claims that Shakespeare's portrayal of Richard III is inaccurate, but the author concludes that this is irrelevant. The author counters that the character is still aesthetically and morally fascinating.

Step 3: Make a Prediction

Note that the author does not dispute the claim of inaccuracy. Instead, the author merely argues that, inaccurate or not, the portrayal is still "fascinating and illuminating both aesthetically and morally." Thus, the author is acting on the principle that aesthetic and/or moral qualities are more important than accuracy.

Step 4: Evaluate the Answer Choices

(A) is correct, matching the author's preference for aesthetics over accuracy.

(B) is a 180. The author argues that accuracy is irrelevant.

(C) is Out of Scope. While it's okay for a principle to be extreme, as this answer is, this principle mistakenly defends Shakespeare based on his "historical importance." The author's defense is based on aesthetic qualities.

(D) is also Out of Scope. Again, although a principle can be extreme, as this answer is, who is responsible for creating history has no effect on the argument of whether accuracy is relevant or not in a historical drama.

(E) is a 180. The author claims inaccuracies are irrelevant, so any reason to correct them would be equally irrelevant.

16. (D) Parallel Flaw

Step 1: Identify the Question Type

The correct answer will be an argument with reasoning "most similar" to that of the original argument. Because that reasoning is described as *flawed*, this is a Parallel Flaw question.

Step 2: Untangle the Stimulus

The voter concludes that the prime minister is seeking a job at an international organization. The evidence is that anyone seeking such a job would spend a lot of time abroad, and the prime minister has been spending a lot of time abroad.

Step 3: Make a Prediction

This is a classic case of confusing necessity and sufficiency. The first claim of evidence is pure Formal Logic. Anyone seeking a job in an international organization spends a lot of time abroad:

> *If*   **seeking int'l org job** →   **spend time abroad**

However, other people could spend time abroad, too. Spending time abroad is not a guarantee, as the voter suggests, that one is seeking a job at an international organization. There could be plenty of other reasons for such travel. The correct answer will commit the same logical error. It will claim that anyone trying to accomplish a particular goal will perform a certain action. It will then conclude that someone performing that action must be trying to accomplish that goal, when there could be plenty of reasons for performing that action.

Step 4: Evaluate the Answer Choices

(D) matches and is correct. It claims that anyone trying to accomplish a particular goal (negotiate a loan) will perform a certain action (go to the bank).

> *If*   **negotiate loan**   →   **go to bank**

It then concludes that Thompson, who is performing that action, must be trying to accomplish the goal. There are plenty of other reasons why someone would go to the bank.

(A) is flawed, but not for the same reason. This illogically claims Kao *must* be a golfer because *most* people in Kao's position play golf. This overlooks the possibility that Kao is not part of the majority, but that's not the same flaw as the original.

(B) does not match. It does not provide any reason to suggest that the logic is flawed. It may overlook some positive

attributes that Franklin may possess, but it does not misinterpret a general claim as the original argument does.

(C) does not match. This makes an unwarranted conclusion about Ramirez having mind control based on what could have been a mere coincidence. This is illogical for sure, but not for the same reason as the original.

(E) does not match. This is flawed in that a lack of evidence against McKinsey does not necessarily indicate guilt. That's like saying the lack of evidence against unicorns suggests that they must be real. Flawed for sure, but not for the same Formal Logic–based reasoning as the original argument.

17. (A) Main Point

Step 1: Identify the Question Type

The correct answer will express the "overall conclusion," or main point, of the argument.

Step 2: Untangle the Stimulus

The first sentence is a strong opinion, suggesting the author's conclusion: debating the truth of the law of noncontradiction is pointless. That law of noncontradiction states that if two statements contradict one another, at least one of those statements must be false. So, why does the author feel debating this law is pointless? The evidence is that … well … who cares? The evidence is a bunch of talking points, and the question is only asking for the conclusion.

Step 3: Make a Prediction

The conclusion is the very first sentence: debating the law of noncontradiction is pointless.

Step 4: Evaluate the Answer Choices

(A) is correct, adequately summarizing the author's main point.

(B) expresses the principle behind the law of noncontradiction. However, that's not the *author's* conclusion. The author's conclusion is that debating that principle is pointless.

(C) is part of the evidence for what makes a debate productive. However, the ensuing evidence describes why that's irrelevant when debating the law of noncontradiction, thus leading to the actual conclusion: such a debate is pointless.

(D) is a Distortion. This takes the requirement for a productive debate and attributes it to the law of noncontradiction. It just mixes and matches random phrases from the argument without any respect for the author's meaning.

(E) is part of the last sentence. However, this lack of certainty is merely part of the evidence why the author concludes that debating the law of noncontradiction is pointless.

18. (B) Flaw

Step 1: Identify the Question Type

The phrase "vulnerable to criticism" is a common indicator of a Flaw question. The correct answer will describe why the argument is flawed.

Step 2: Untangle the Stimulus

The pundit concludes that attending a university would be useless for getting a corporate job. The evidence is that corporations value a certain set of skills that many high school graduates already have without going to college.

Step 3: Make a Prediction

The key to recognizing the flaw here is to notice the overly strong language in the conclusion: attending a university would be "of no help" in finding a corporate job. This ignores the possibility that there is *some* benefit. Even if high students already possess some of the most sought-after skills, there could still be *something* that universities provide that high school wouldn't. The correct answer will point out this overlooked possibility.

Step 4: Evaluate the Answer Choices

(B) is correct, pointing out an overlooked benefit to college. Even if high school graduates possess the most sought-after skills, there could still be *some* skill required that only attending a university could provide.

(A) is a 180. University graduates *would* have those skills, but they already would have had them after high school. The pundit's argument still stands that college would be unnecessary.

(C) is Extreme. The pundit never claims or assumes that corporations hire *only* people with those skills. It's merely said that corporations value those skills the most.

(D) is irrelevant. The pundit's argument is merely that universities are of no help "in getting a corporate job." The pundit is not dismissing universities for other purposes, and thus does not assume that there's no other reason to attend a university.

(E) is irrelevant. It doesn't matter how students acquire those skills, whether through study or firsthand experience. All that matters is that they acquire those skills by the time they've graduated high school.

19. (B) Weaken

Step 1: Identify the Question Type

The question directly asks for something that will weaken the argument.

Step 2: Untangle the Stimulus

The archaeologist concludes that Neanderthals probably preserved meat by smoking it. The evidence is the presence of burnt lichen and grass, which produce a lot of smoke but not as much heat or light as wood.

Step 3: Make a Prediction

The archaeologist is making two assumptions. First, the archaeologist assumes that the smoke created by the lichen and grass was used for smoking meat, and for no other reason. Second, the archaeologist assumes that the light and heat produced by lichen and grass was not good enough for Neanderthals, i.e., they would have used wood (or something similar) if they really wanted light and heat. The correct answer will contradict one, if not both, of these assumptions by suggesting that the lichen and grass was used for another reason or that it provided enough heat and light.

Step 4: Evaluate the Answer Choices

(B) is correct. Wood might make for a warmer, brighter fire if it was available. But if it wasn't, and nothing in the area was better than lichen and grass, then it's possible the lichen and grass were used for heat and light and not for smoking meats.

(A) is a 180. If there were other fireplaces that were used to produce more heat, then the fireplaces with the lichen and grass were probably used to produce smoke, which would only strengthen the archaeologist's view.

(C) is a 180, indicating that Neanderthals went to great lengths to procure lichens. This suggests that it was important to have a smoke-producing substance, thus strengthening the archaeologist's view.

(D) is Out of Scope. The archaeologist is not claiming that *all* Neanderthals preserved all of their meat by smoking it. Even if there were some later Neanderthals that developed an alternative method for some of their meat, the archaeologist's argument still stands.

(E) is a 180. This offers a reason why smoking meat would be beneficial, thus adding support to the archaeologist's claim.

20. (B) Point at Issue

Step 1: Identify the Question Type

The correct answer will be what two speakers, Edgar and Rafaela, "disagree over," making this a Point at Issue question.

Step 2: Untangle the Stimulus

Edgar argues that it's absurd to shut down some of the regional pumps. He claims the shutdown is all about saving one species of fish, but that's not worth inconveniencing thousands of people. Rafaela, however, argues there's another purpose to shutting down the pumps. If the fish are threatened, then so is the water supply. The fish are merely an indicator of a larger problem.

Step 3: Make a Prediction

Edgar and Rafaela surely disagree about shutting down the pumps. Edgar argues that they should not be shut down, but Rafaela is suggesting that they should be shut down. However, this disagreement stems from a bigger issue. Edgar believes the shutdown is all about saving the fish. Rafaela believes there's more to the shutdown than just one fish species. The correct answer will address the conflicting view on shutting down the pumps or the conflicting view on the motive for shutting down the pumps.

Step 4: Evaluate the Answer Choices

(B) is correct. Edgar would agree with this, saying the pumps are being shut down solely to save the fish. Rafaela would disagree, arguing that there's a greater purpose that involves protecting the water supply.

(A) is not supported. Edgar agrees that people will be inconvenienced, but Rafaela does not dispute that claim. Rafaela only weighs in on the reason why such drastic measures are being taken.

(C) is not supported. Edgar agrees that these specific small fish are inconsequential, but Rafaela does not dispute that. Instead, Rafaela merely emphasizes a greater motive behind the shutdown.

(D) is not supported. Neither speaker addresses the legality of shutting down the pipes.

(E) is not supported. Neither Edgar nor Rafaela address whether the fish will actually be saved or not. The debate is over whether or not the fish are the primary motivation for shutting down the pumps.

21. (C) Assumption (Necessary)

Step 1: Identify the Question Type

The question asks for an "assumption required," making this a Necessary Assumption question. However, unlike most assumptions that are used to plug up holes in an argument, this assumption will plug up a hole in an analogy.

Step 2: Untangle the Stimulus

The author starts by drawing a distinction between engineering and two other sciences, physics and chemistry. Engineering can see how a machine works and analyze the nature of that machine. Physics and chemistry can only describe the physical conditions behind the machine's success, but cannot describe the machine's purpose. The author then makes an analogy to a distinction between physiology and the same two sciences. Physiology can see how an organism functions and analyze the nature of that organism. Physics and chemistry cannot determine those functions.

Step 3: Make a Prediction

Both parts of the analogy raise the inability of physics and chemistry to determine the function or purpose of something. However, both parts of the analogy compare physics and chemistry to two totally different fields: engineering and physiology. For this analogy to work, engineering and physiology must be comparable in some relevant sense.

Step 4: Evaluate the Answer Choices

(C) must be assumed. Using the Denial Test, if there were no connection between engineers' notions about machinery and physiologists' notions about organisms, the entire analogy would fall apart.

(A) is a Distortion. It's only important that the way physiologists *analyze* organisms is comparable to how engineers *analyze* machinery. The organisms and machines themselves do not need to be similar.

(B) is not necessary. This just takes the wording used for physics and chemistry in the engineering analogy and repeats it with physiological terms. However, the physics and chemistry part of the analogy was never an issue. The problem is the disconnect between engineering and physiology, and this answer makes no connection.

(D) is a Distortion. The analogy emphasizes how physics and chemistry differ from other fields, but never claims these fields are "largely independent" of one another. Engineering was never said to be "largely independent" of physics and chemistry, so physiology need not be either.

(E) is Extreme. In the engineering analogy, the author never claims that machines *cannot* be reduced to mechanical or chemical processes. On the contrary, they *can*. It's just that physics and chemistry cannot express *purpose*. Therefore, the author need not assume biological process cannot be reduced to mechanical or chemical processes. They *can*, but physics and chemistry cannot express the operational principles.

22. (C) Strengthen

Step 1: Identify the Question Type

The question directly asks for something that strengthens the argument.

Step 2: Untangle the Stimulus

The author concludes (*therefore*) that the hepadnavirus is at least 25 million years old. The evidence is that the hepadnavirus inserts itself into an animal's chromosome and then gets passed down from generation to generation. One hepadnavirus fragment is found in chromosomes of both zebra finches and juncos, bird species that diverged from each other 25 million years ago. In addition, the virus fragment is found in the exact same location in corresponding chromosomes.

Step 3: Make a Prediction

The author is suggesting that the virus inserted itself into a bird at least 25 million years ago. It was genetically passed down until 25 million years ago, when that bird species diverged into two separate birds: zebra finches and juncos. The strongest evidence is the placement of the virus. Both birds have the virus in the exact same location in a similar chromosome. It can't be a coincidence … or could it? Maybe the virus always inserts itself in the same location of a chromosome. If that were true, the virus could have inserted itself at two different times, perhaps just 1,000 years ago. The author assumes otherwise: the virus inserted itself once at least 25 million years ago, and the identical placement is not a coincidence. The correct answer will verify this assumption.

Step 4: Evaluate the Answer Choices

(C) is correct, validating the assumption that the virus inserted itself just once. If the placement of the virus is always random, it would be too coincidental that the virus was found in the *exact same spot* in both birds' chromosomes. It makes it much more likely that it was inserted once over 25 million years ago and got passed along during the split.

(A) is a Distortion. Even if viruses did have this ability, there's no evidence that the split wasn't caused by a different virus and the hepadnavirus inserted itself at different, much more recent times.

(B) is irrelevant. Even if no other viruses are present, there's still no evidence that the hepadnavirus fragments are genetically linked to the same virus from before the species diverged.

(D) is Out of Scope. There would still be the question of whether those fragments appear in the very same spot in those birds' chromosomes. If they did, then the author's argument seems less valid because if unrelated bird species all have the virus show up in the same spot of the chromosome, then the placement of the virus is not random, and thus, the zebra finch and dark-eyed junco need not have both had the virus at the time of their split. They could have each contracted the virus at different times much more recently than 25 million years ago.

(E) is also Out of Scope. Even if the hepadnavirus doesn't affect a species' survival, there's still no evidence that the same virus inserted itself into a bird 25 million years ago.

23. (B) Inference

Step 1: Identify the Question Type

The correct answer will be "properly inferred from the statements" given, making this an Inference question.

Step 2: Untangle the Stimulus

The *H. subflexa* caterpillar eats only one thing: a particular fruit that lacks linolenic acid. Many other insects require linolenic acid to grow and mature. Linolenic acid also needs to be consumed to produce a chemical called volicitin. Most caterpillars produce volicitin, but *H. subflexa* does not.

Step 3: Make a Prediction

There's a lot of information provided. However, when asked for something *properly* inferred, look for the most absolute statements with the most Formal Logic. Then find ways of combining that information.

There's not much to be said about the *H.subflexa* caterpillar. Unlike many other insects, it does not ingest linolenic acid, and unlike other caterpillars, it doesn't produce volicitin. However, there's not much to deduce from those statements. On the other hand, linolenic acid is said to be *necessary* for two things. In many insects, it's necessary for growth. It also needs to be consumed to produce volicitin. Further, volicitin is produced in *most* caterpillars. If most caterpillars produce volicitin, and producing volicitin requires consuming linolenic acid, then most caterpillars must consume linolenic acid. Test the answers, making sure that the correct one is absolutely true based on the logic.

Step 4: Evaluate the Answer Choices

(B) must be true, and is thus correct. Most caterpillars produce volicitin, and that requires a diet that includes linolenic acid. Thus, most caterpillars must consume linolenic acid.

(A) is not supported. *H. subflexa* does not consume linolenic acid, but it doesn't need to. *Other* insects are said to need linolenic acid to grow. And *H. subflexa* does not produce volicitin. Therefore, *H. subflexa* has no stated need for linolenic acid, and there's no guarantee that it creates its own linolenic acid.

(C) is a Distortion of the Formal Logic. Linolenic acid is *necessary* to produce volicitin, but it's not *sufficient*. The caterpillars that produce volicitin must consume linolenic acid, but there may be other caterpillars that consume linolenic acid *without* producing volicitin.

(D) is unsupported. While *H. subflexa* caterpillars eat only one thing that doesn't have linolenic acid, that doesn't mean linolenic acid would be *poisonous*.

(E) is not supported. While most caterpillars need the linolenic acid absent from *Physalis* fruit, there could be plenty of other caterpillars that eat that fruit along with *H. subflexa*. Even the ones that do need linolenic acid could eat that fruit, too. They would just need to eat other foods as well.

24. (B) Role of a Statement

Step 1: Identify the Question Type

The question provides a claim from the stimulus and asks for the "role played in the argument" by that claim. That makes this a Role of a Statement question.

Step 2: Untangle the Stimulus

The politician starts with a requirement for democracy: people must be able to share ideas freely. That leads to the conclusion ([*t*]*herefore*) that the right to have unmonitored private conversations is essential to democracy. That, in turn, leads to the final conclusion (*thus*) that monitoring Internet conversations would be bad for democracy. Said differently, the politician concludes government monitoring of Internet conversations would be bad. Why? Because unmonitored conversations are essential to democracy. Why? Because democracy requires no restrictions on free sharing of ideas.

Step 3: Make a Prediction

The argument has a very basic structure. There's an opening claim, followed by a conclusion. That conclusion is then used as evidence to back up the final conclusion. So, in order, there's a claim, a subsidiary conclusion, and the main conclusion. The question asks for the role of the first statement. That's the claim that backs up the subsidiary conclusion.

Step 4: Evaluate the Answer Choices

(B) correctly identifies the first statement as a claim that supports another claim, which further supports the main conclusion. In other words, it's a claim that supports a subsidiary conclusion.

(A) is a Distortion. The first statement does support *a* conclusion, but not directly the *main* conclusion. If the first statement is said to support the main conclusion, then it only does so indirectly by supporting another conclusion first. It does not support *only* the main conclusion.

(C) is a 180. There is no support for the opening sentence. It is just an accepted claim that is used as evidence.

(D) is mistaken. The main conclusion is the last sentence, not the first. The first statement is not inferred from anything.

(E) is mistaken. The main conclusion is the last sentence, not the first. The first statement is not inferred from anything. Furthermore, the two other statements *are* used—one in support of the other. The second sentence supports the third sentence.

25. (C) Inference

Step 1: Identify the Question Type

The correct answer will be "strongly supported" by the information provided. That makes this an Inference question.

Step 2: Untangle the Stimulus

The author starts out by claiming that you can compare two chess-playing programs by seeing how each one performs under time restraints. How do you compare these programs? The author never says, so that's unknown. Instead, the author suddenly shifts scope and starts talking about comparing *computers*. If you test the same program on two different computers, the faster computer will more likely win because it can examine more moves within the time limit.

Step 3: Make a Prediction

The key to answering this question is to not be thrown by the first sentence. The first sentence suggests that there's a way to compare chess-playing programs, but it never actually says how. It just says that you *can*. All that's really mentioned is how to compare two computers. The faster computer can examine more moves in a given time limit, so the author claims the faster computer is more likely to win. That implies that the number of moves one can examine within a given time limit somehow affects one's ability to win.

Step 4: Evaluate the Answer Choices

(C) is directly supported. Faster computers are said to have a better chance of winning *because* they can examine more moves in any given time frame. Thus, under a given time constraint, more examining means a better chance of winning.

(A) is not supported. The author never discusses the criteria for comparing two programs. The only criterion provided is for how to compare two computers: whichever one works faster is better. It's possible that a program that tests fewer moves is still better because it's been better programmed to test more effective moves first.

(B) is not supported. Speed can be a factor in determining which computer is more likely to win, but there's no information about compatibility or the ability to run a particular program.

(D) is not supported. If the *same* program were running on two different computers, the faster computer would be able to test more moves. However, if it's two *different* programs, the results are unknown. Maybe the coding of the program on the faster computer is far more complex. In that case, the faster computer may still not be able to examine as many moves due to the nature of the program.

(E) is not supported. Raising the time limit on the slower computer would certainly allow it to examine more moves than it could previously. However, it depends entirely on how much you raise the time limit. If you only raise it a little, the faster computer might still be able to examine more moves and still have a better chance of winning. If you raise it a lot, you may allow the slower computer to examine many more moves and gain the upper hand. There's no guarantee of perfectly hitting the time limit that allows for an "equal chance of winning."

Glossary

Logical Reasoning

Logical Reasoning Question Types

Argument-Based Questions

Main Point Question

A question that asks for an argument's conclusion or an author's main point. Typical question stems:

> Which one the following most accurately expresses the conclusion of the argument as a whole?

> Which one of the following sentences best expresses the main point of the scientist's argument?

Role of a Statement Question

A question that asks how a specific sentence, statement, or idea functions within an argument. Typical question stems:

> Which one of the following most accurately describes the role played in the argument by the statement that automation within the steel industry allowed steel mills to produce more steel with fewer workers?

> The claim that governmental transparency is a nation's primary defense against public-sector corruption figures in the argument in which one of the following ways?

Point at Issue Question

A question that asks you to identify the specific claim, statement, or recommendation about which two speakers/authors disagree (or, rarely, about which they agree). Typical question stems:

> A point at issue between Tom and Jerry is

> The dialogue most strongly supports the claim that Marilyn and Billy disagree with each other about which one of the following?

Method of Argument Question

A question that asks you to describe an author's argumentative strategy. In other words, the correct answer describes *how* the author argues (not necessarily what the author says). Typical question stems:

> Which one of the following most accurately describes the technique of reasoning employed by the argument?

> Julian's argument proceeds by

> In the dialogue, Alexander responds to Abigail in which one of the following ways?

Parallel Reasoning Question

A question that asks you to identify the answer choice containing an argument that has the same logical structure and reaches the same type of conclusion as the argument in the stimulus does. Typical question stems:

> The pattern of reasoning in which one of the following arguments is most parallel to that in the argument above?

> The pattern of reasoning in which one of the following arguments is most similar to the pattern of reasoning in the argument above?

Assumption-Family Questions

Assumption Question

A question that asks you to identify one of the unstated premises in an author's argument. Assumption questions come in two varieties.

Necessary Assumption questions ask you to identify an unstated premise required for an argument's conclusion to follow logically from its evidence. Typical question stems:

> Which one of the following is an assumption on which the argument depends?

> Which one of the following is an assumption that the argument requires in order for its conclusion to be properly drawn?

Sufficient Assumption questions ask you to identify an unstated premise sufficient to establish the argument's conclusion on the basis of its evidence. Typical question stems:

> The conclusion follows logically if which one of the following is assumed?

> Which one of the following, if assumed, enables the conclusion above to be properly inferred?

Strengthen/Weaken Question

A question that asks you to identify a fact that, if true, would make the argument's conclusion more likely (Strengthen) or less likely (Weaken) to follow from its evidence. Typical question stems:

Strengthen

> Which one of the following, if true, most strengthens the argument above?

> Which one the following, if true, most strongly supports the claim above?

Weaken

> Which one of the following, if true, would most weaken the argument above?

> Which one of the following, if true, most calls into question the claim above?

Flaw Question

A question that asks you to describe the reasoning error that the author has made in an argument. Typical question stems:

The argument's reasoning is most vulnerable to criticism on the grounds that the argument

Which of the following identifies a reasoning error in the argument?

The reasoning in the correspondent's argument is questionable because the argument

Parallel Flaw Question

A question that asks you to identify the argument that contains the same error(s) in reasoning that the argument in the stimulus contains. Typical question stems:

The pattern of flawed reasoning exhibited by the argument above is most similar to that exhibited in which one of the following?

Which one of the following most closely parallels the questionable reasoning cited above?

Evaluate the Argument Question

A question that asks you to identify an issue or consideration relevant to the validity of an argument. Think of Evaluate questions as "Strengthen or Weaken" questions. The correct answer, if true, will strengthen the argument, and if false, will weaken the argument, or vice versa. Evaluate questions are very rare. Typical question stems:

Which one of the following would be most useful to know in order to evaluate the legitimacy of the professor's argument?

It would be most important to determine which one of the following in evaluating the argument?

Non-Argument Questions

Inference Question

A question that asks you to identify a statement that follows from the statements in the stimulus. It is very important to note the characteristics of the one correct and the four incorrect answers before evaluating the choices in Inference questions. Depending on the wording of the question stem, the correct answer to an Inference question may be the one that

- *must be true* if the statements in the stimulus are true

- is *most strongly supported* by the statements in the stimulus

- *must be false* if the statements in the stimulus are true

Typical question stems:

If all of the statements above are true, then which one of the following must also be true?

Which one of the following can be properly inferred from the information above?

If the statements above are true, then each of the following could be true EXCEPT:

Which one of the following is most strongly supported by the information above?

The statements above, if true, most support which one of the following?

The facts described above provide the strongest evidence against which one of the following?

Paradox Question

A question that asks you to identify a fact that, if true, most helps to explain, resolve, or reconcile an apparent contradiction. Typical question stems:

Which one of the following, if true, most helps to explain how both studies' findings could be accurate?

Which one the following, if true, most helps to resolve the apparent conflict in the spokesperson's statements?

Each one of the following, if true, would contribute to an explanation of the apparent discrepancy in the information above EXCEPT:

Principle Questions

Principle Question

A question that asks you to identify corresponding cases and principles. Some Principle questions provide a principle in the stimulus and call for the answer choice describing a case that corresponds to the principle. Others provide a specific case in the stimulus and call for the answer containing a principle to which that case corresponds.

On the LSAT, Principle questions almost always mirror the skills rewarded by other Logical Reasoning question types. After each of the following Principle question stems, we note the question type it resembles. Typical question stems:

Which one of the following principles, if valid, most helps to justify the reasoning above? (**Strengthen**)

Which one of the following most accurately expresses the principle underlying the reasoning above? (**Assumption**)

The situation described above most closely conforms to which of the following generalizations? (**Inference**)

Which one of the following situations conforms most closely to the principle described above? (**Inference**)

Which one of the following principles, if valid, most helps to reconcile the apparent conflict among the prosecutor's claims? (**Paradox**)

Parallel Principle Question

A question that asks you to identify a specific case that illustrates the same principle that is illustrated by the case described in the stimulus. Typical question stem:

Of the following, which one illustrates a principle that is most similar to the principle illustrated by the passage?

Untangling the Stimulus

Conclusion Types

The conclusions in arguments found in the Logical Reasoning section of the LSAT tend to fall into one of six categories:

1) Value Judgment (an evaluative statement; e.g., Action X is unethical, or Y's recital was poorly sung)

2) "If"/Then (a conditional prediction, recommendation, or assertion; e.g., If X is true, then so is Y, or If you an M, then you should do N)

3) Prediction (X *will* or *will not* happen in the future)

4) Comparison (X is taller/shorter/more common/less common, etc. than Y)

5) Assertion of Fact (X is true or X is false)

6) Recommendation (we *should* or *should not* do X)

One-Sentence Test

A tactic used to identify the author's conclusion in an argument. Consider which sentence in the argument is the one the author would keep if asked to get rid of everything except her main point.

Subsidiary Conclusion

A conclusion following from one piece of evidence and then used by the author to support his overall conclusion or main point. Consider the following argument:

> The pharmaceutical company's new experimental treatment did not succeed in clinical trials. As a result, the new treatment will not reach the market this year. Thus, the company will fall short of its revenue forecasts for the year.

Here, the sentence "As a result, the new treatment will not reach the market this year" is a subsidiary conclusion. It follows from the evidence that the new treatment failed in clinical trials, and it provides evidence for the overall conclusion that the company will not meet its revenue projections.

Keyword(s) in Logical Reasoning

A word or phrase that helps you untangle a question's stimulus by indicating the logical structure of the argument or the author's point. Here are three categories of Keywords to which LSAT experts pay special attention in Logical Reasoning:

Conclusion words; e.g., *therefore, thus, so, as a result, it follows that, consequently,* [evidence] *is evidence that* [conclusion]

Evidence word; e.g, *because, since, after all, for,* [evidence] *is evidence that* [conclusion]

Contrast words; e.g., *but, however, while, despite, in spite of, on the other hand* (These are especially useful in Paradox and Inference questions.)

Experts use Keywords even more extensively in Reading Comprehension. Learn the Keywords associated with the Reading Comprehension section, and apply them to Logical Reasoning when they are helpful.

Mismatched Concepts

One of two patterns to which authors' assumptions conform in LSAT arguments. Mismatched Concepts describes the assumption in arguments in which terms or concepts in the conclusion are different *in kind* from those in the evidence. The author assumes that there is a logical relationship between the different terms. For example:

> Bobby is a **championship swimmer**. Therefore, he **trains every day**.

Here, the words "trains every day" appear only in the conclusion, and the words "championship swimmer" appear only in the evidence. For the author to reach this conclusion from this evidence, he assumes that championship swimmers train every day.

Another example:

> Susan does **not eat her vegetables**. Thus, she will **not grow big and strong**.

In this argument, not growing big and strong is found only in the conclusion while not eating vegetables is found only in the evidence. For the author to reach this conclusion from this evidence, she must assume that eating one's vegetables is necessary for one to grow big and strong.

See also Overlooked Possibilities.

Overlooked Possibilities

One of two patterns to which authors' assumptions conform in LSAT arguments. Mismatched Concepts describes the assumption in arguments in which terms or concepts in the conclusion are different *in degree, scale, or level of certainty* from those in the evidence. The author assumes that there is no factor or explanation for the conclusion other than the one(s) offered in the evidence. For example:

> Samson does not have a ticket stub for this movie showing. Thus, Samson must have sneaked into the movie without paying.

The author assumes that there is no other explanation for Samson's lack of a ticket stub. The author overlooks several possibilities: e.g., Samson had a special pass for this showing of the movie; Samson dropped his ticket stub by accident or threw it away after entering the theater; someone else in Samson's party has all of the party members' ticket stubs in her pocket or handbag.

Another example:

> Jonah's marketing plan will save the company money. Therefore, the company should adopt Jonah's plan.

Here, the author makes a recommendation based on one advantage. The author assumes that the advantage is the company's only concern or that there are no disadvantages that could outweigh it, e.g., Jonah's plan might save money on marketing but not generate any new leads or customers; Jonah's plan might damage the company's image or reputation; Jonah's plan might include illegal false advertising. Whenever the author of an LSAT argument concludes with a recommendation or a prediction based on just a single fact in the evidence, that author is always overlooking many other possibilities.

See also Mismatched Concepts.

Causal Argument

An argument in which the author concludes or assumes that one thing causes another. The most common pattern on the LSAT is for the author to conclude that A causes B from evidence that A and B are correlated. For example:

> I notice that whenever the store has a poor sales month, employee tardiness is also higher that month. Therefore, it must be that employee tardiness causes the store to lose sales.

The author assumes that the correlation in the evidence indicates a causal relationship. These arguments are vulnerable to three types of overlooked possibilities:

1) There could be **another causal factor**. In the previous example, maybe the months in question are those in which the manager takes vacation, causing the store to lose sales and permitting employees to arrive late without fear of the boss's reprimands.

2) Causation could be **reversed**. Maybe in months when sales are down, employee morale suffers and tardiness increases as a result.

3) The correlation could be **coincidental**. Maybe the correlation between tardiness and the dip in sales is pure coincidence.

See also Flaw Types: Correlation versus Causation.

Another pattern in causal arguments (less frequent on the LSAT) involves the assumption that a particular causal mechanism is or is not involved in a causal relationship. For example:

> The airport has rerouted takeoffs and landings so that they will not create noise over the Sunnyside neighborhood. Thus, the recent drop in Sunnyside's property values cannot be explained by the neighborhood's proximity to the airport.

Here, the author assumes that the only way that the airport could be the cause of dropping property values is through noise pollution. The author overlooks any other possible mechanism (e.g., frequent traffic jams and congestion) through which proximity to the airport could be cause of Sunnyside's woes.

Principle

A broad, law-like rule, definition, or generalization that covers a variety of specific cases with defined attributes. To see how principles are treated on the LSAT, consider the following principle:

> It is immoral for a person for his own gain to mislead another person.

That principle would cover a specific case, such as a seller who lies about the quality of construction to get a higher price for his house. It would also correspond to the case of a teenager who, wishing to spend a night out on the town, tells his mom "I'm going over to Randy's house." He knows that his mom believes that he will be staying at Randy's house, when in fact, he and Randy will go out together.

That principle does not, however, cover cases in which someone lies solely for the purpose of making the other person feel better or in which one person inadvertently misleads the other through a mistake of fact.

Be careful not to apply your personal ethics or morals when analyzing the principles articulated on the test.

Flaw Types

Necessary versus Sufficient

This flaw occurs when a speaker or author concludes that one event is necessary for a second event from evidence that the first event is sufficient to bring about the second event, or vice versa. Example:

> If more than 25,000 users attempt to access the new app at the same time, the server will crash. Last night, at 11:15 pm, the server crashed, so it must be case that more than 25,000 users were attempting to use the new app at that time.

In making this argument, the author assumes that the only thing that will cause the server to crash is the usage level (i.e., high usage is *necessary* for the server to crash). The evidence, however, says that high usage is one thing that will cause the server to crash (i.e., that high usage is *sufficient* to crash the server).

Correlation versus Causation

This flaw occurs when a speaker or author draws a conclusion that one thing causes another from evidence that the two things are correlated. Example:

Over the past half century, global sugar consumption has tripled. That same time period has seen a surge in the rate of technological advancement worldwide. It follows that the increase in sugar consumption has caused the acceleration in technological advancement.

In any argument with this structure, the author is making three unwarranted assumptions. First, he assumes that there is no alternate cause, i.e., there is nothing else that has contributed to rapid technological advancement. Second, he assumes that the causation is not reversed, i.e., technological advancement has not contributed to the increase in sugar consumption, perhaps by making it easier to grow, refine, or transport sugar. And, third, he assumes that the two phenomena are not merely coincidental, i.e., that it is not just happenstance that global sugar consumption is up at the same time that the pace of technological advancement has accelerated.

Unrepresentative Sample

This flaw occurs when a speaker or author draws a conclusion about a group from evidence in which the sample cannot represent that group because the sample is too small or too selective, or is biased in some way. Example:

Moviegoers in our town prefer action films and romantic comedies over other film genres. Last Friday, we sent reporters to survey moviegoers at several theaters in town, and nearly 90 percent of those surveyed were going to watch either an action film or a romantic comedy.

The author assumes that the survey was representative of the town's moviegoers, but there are several reasons to question that assumption. First, we don't know how many people were actually surveyed. Even if the number of people surveyed was adequate, we don't know how many other types of movies were playing. Finally, the author doesn't limit her conclusion to moviegoers on Friday nights. If the survey had been conducted at Sunday matinees, maybe most moviegoers would have been heading out to see an animated family film or a historical drama. Who knows?

Scope Shift/Unwarranted Assumption

This flaw occurs when a speaker's or author's evidence has a scope or has terms different enough from the scope or terms in his conclusion that it is doubtful that the evidence can support the conclusion. Example:

A very small percentage of working adults in this country can correctly define collateralized debt obligation securities. Thus, sad to say, the majority of the nation's working adults cannot make prudent choices about how to invest their savings.

This speaker assumes that prudent investing requires the ability to accurately define a somewhat obscure financial term. But prudence is not the same thing as expertise, and the speaker does not offer any evidence that this knowledge of this particular term is related to wise investing.

Percent versus Number/Rate versus Number

This flaw occurs when a speaker or author draws a conclusion about real quantities from evidence about rates or percentages, or vice versa. Example:

At the end of last season, Camp SunnyDay laid off half of their senior counselors and a quarter of their junior counselors. Thus, Camp SunnyDay must have more senior counselors than junior counselors.

The problem, of course, is that we don't know how many senior and junior counselors were on staff before the layoffs. If there were a total of 4 senior counselors and 20 junior counselors, then the camp would have laid off only 2 senior counselors while dismissing 5 junior counselors.

Equivocation

This flaw occurs when a speaker or author uses the same word in two different and incompatible ways. Example:

Our opponent in the race has accused our candidate's staff members of behaving unprofessionally. But that's not fair. Our staff is made up entirely of volunteers, not paid campaign workers.

The speaker interprets the opponent's use of the word *professional* to mean "paid," but the opponent likely meant something more along the lines of "mature, competent, and businesslike."

Ad Hominem

This flaw occurs when a speaker or author concludes that another person's claim or argument is invalid because that other person has a personal flaw or shortcoming. One common pattern is for the speaker or author to claim the other person acts hypocritically or that the other person's claim is made from self-interest. Example:

Mrs. Smithers testified before the city council, stating that the speed limits on the residential streets near her home are dangerously high. But why should we give her claim any credence? The way she eats and exercises, she's not even looking out for her own health.

The author attempts to undermine Mrs. Smithers's testimony by attacking her character and habits. He doesn't offer any evidence that is relevant to her claim about speed limits.

Part versus Whole

This flaw occurs when a speaker or author concludes that a part or individual has a certain characteristic because the whole or the larger group has that characteristic, or vice versa. Example:

Patient: I should have no problems taking the three drugs prescribed to me by my doctors. I looked them up, and none of the three is listed as having any major side effects.

Here, the patient is assuming that what is true of each of the drugs individually will be true of them when taken together. The patient's flaw is overlooking possible interactions that could cause problems not present when the drugs are taken separately.

Circular Reasoning

This flaw occurs when a speaker or author tries to prove a conclusion with evidence that is logically equivalent to the conclusion. Example:

> All those who run for office are prevaricators. To   see this, just consider politicians: they all prevaricate.

Perhaps the author has tried to disguise the circular reasoning in this argument by exchanging the words "those who run for office" in the conclusion for "politicians" in the evidence, but all this argument amounts to is "Politicians prevaricate; therefore, politicians prevaricate." On the LSAT, circular reasoning is very rarely the correct answer to a Flaw question, although it is regularly described in one of the wrong answers.

Question Strategies

Denial Test

A tactic for identifying the assumption *necessary* to an argument. When you negate an assumption necessary to an argument, the argument will fall apart. Negating an assumption that is not necessary to the argument will not invalidate the argument. Consider the following argument:

> Only high schools which produced a state champion athlete during the school year will be represented at the Governor's awards banquet. Therefore, McMurtry High School will be represented at the Governor's awards banquet.

Which one of the following is an assumption necessary to that argument?

(1) McMurtry High School produced more state champion athletes than any other high school during the school year.

(2) McMurtry High School produced at least one state champion athlete during the school year.

If you are at all confused about which of those two statements reflects the *necessary* assumption, negate them both.

(1) McMurtry High School **did not produce more** state champion athletes than any other high school during the school year.

That does not invalidate the argument. McMurtry could still be represented at the Governor's banquet.

(2) McMurtry High School **did not produce any** state champion athletes during the school year.

Here, negating the statement causes the argument to fall apart. Statement (2) is an assumption *necessary* to the argument.

Point at Issue "Decision Tree"

A tactic for evaluating the answer choices in Point at Issue questions. The correct answer is the only answer choice to which you can answer "Yes" to all three questions in the following diagram.

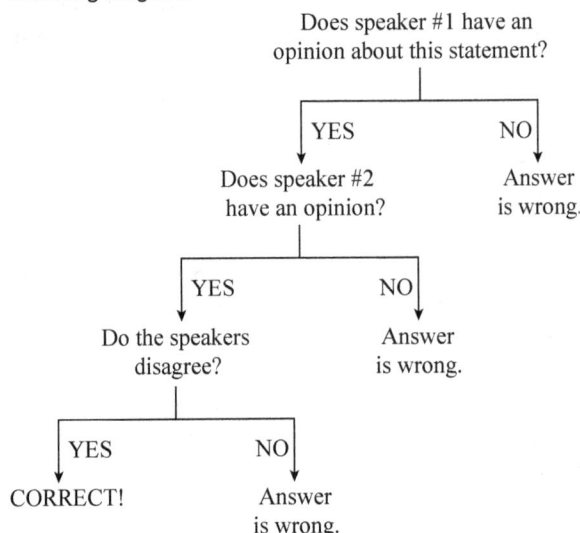

Common Methods of Argument

These methods of argument or argumentative strategies are common on the LSAT:

- Analogy, in which an author draws parallels between two unrelated (but purportedly similar) situations
- Example, in which an author cites a specific case or cases to justify a generalization
- Counterexample, in which an author seeks to discredit an opponent's argument by citing a specific case or cases that appear to invalidate the opponent's generalization
- Appeal to authority, in which an author cites an expert's claim or opinion as support for her conclusion
- Ad hominem attack, in which an author attacks her opponent's personal credibility rather than attacking the substance of her opponent's argument
- Elimination of alternatives, in which an author lists possibilities and discredits or rules out all but one

- Means/requirements, in which the author argues that something is needed to achieve a desired result

Wrong Answer Types in LR

Outside the Scope (Out of Scope; Beyond the Scope)

An answer choice containing a statement that is too broad, too narrow, or beyond the purview of the stimulus, making the statement in the choice irrelevant

180

An answer choice that directly contradicts what the correct answer must say (for example, a choice that strengthens the argument in a Weaken question)

Extreme

An answer choice containing language too emphatic to be supported by the stimulus; often (although not always) characterized by words such as *all*, *never*, *every*, *only*, or *most*

Distortion

An answer choice that mentions details from the stimulus but mangles or misstates what the author said about those details

Irrelevant Comparison

An answer choice that compares two items or attributes in a way not germane to the author's argument or statements

Half-Right/Half-Wrong

An answer choice that begins correctly, but then contradicts or distorts the passage in its second part; this wrong answer type is more common in Reading Comprehension than it is in Logical Reasoning

Faulty Use of Detail

An answer choice that accurately states something from the stimulus, but does so in a manner that answers the question incorrectly; this wrong answer type is more common in Reading Comprehension than it is in Logical Reasoning

Logic Games

Game Types

Strict Sequencing Game

A game that asks you to arrange entities into numbered positions or into a set schedule (usually hours or days). Strict Sequencing is, by far, the most common game type on the LSAT. In the typical Strict Sequencing game, there is a one-to-one matchup of entities and positions, e.g., seven entities to be placed in seven positions, one per position, or six entities to be placed over six consecutive days, one entity per day.

From time to time, the LSAT will offer Strict Sequencing with more entities than positions (e.g., seven entities to be arranged over five days, with some days to receive more than one entity) or more positions than entities (e.g., six entities to be scheduled over seven days, with at least one day to receive no entities).

Other, less common variations on Strict Sequencing include:

Double Sequencing, in which each entity is placed or scheduled two times (there have been rare occurrences of Triple or Quadruple Sequencing). Alternatively, a Double Sequencing game may involve two different sets of entities each sequenced once.

Circular Sequencing, in which entities are arranged around a table or in a circular arrangement (NOTE: When the positions in a Circular Sequencing game are numbered, the first and last positions are adjacent.)

Vertical Sequencing, in which the positions are numbered from top to bottom or from bottom to top (as in the floors of a building)

Loose Sequencing Game

A game that asks you to arrange or schedule entities in order but provides no numbering or naming of the positions. The rules in Loose Sequencing give only the relative positions (earlier or later, higher or lower) between two entities or among three entities. Loose Sequencing games almost always provide that there will be no ties between entities in the rank, order, or position they take.

Circular Sequencing Game

See Strict Sequencing Game.

Selection Game

A game that asks you to choose or include some entities from the initial list of entities and to reject or exclude others. Some Selection games provide overall limitations on the number of entities to be selected (e.g., "choose exactly four of seven students" or "choose at least two of six entrees") while others provide little or no restriction on the number selected ("choose at least one type of flower" or "select from among seven board members").

Distribution Game

A game that asks you to break up the initial list of entities into two, three, or (very rarely) four groups or teams. In the vast majority of Distribution games, each entity is assigned to one and only one group or team. A relatively common variation on Distribution games will provide a subdivided list of entities (e.g., eight students—four men and four women—will form three study groups) and will then require representatives from those subdivisions on each team (e.g., each study group will have at least one of the men on it).

Matching Game

A game that asks you to match one or more members of one set of entities to specific members of another set of entities, or that asks you to match attributes or objects to a set of entities. Unlike Distribution games, in which each entity is placed in exactly one group or team, Matching games usually permit you to assign the same attribute or object to more than one entity.

In some cases, there are overall limitations on the number of entities that can be matched (e.g., "In a school's wood shop, there are four workstations—numbered 1 through 4—and each workstation has at least one and at most three of the following tools—band saw, dremmel tool, electric sander, and power drill"). In almost all Matching games, further restrictions on the number of entities that can be matched to a particular person or place will be found in the rules (e.g., Workstation 4 will have more tools than Workstation 2 has).

Hybrid Game

A game that asks you to do two (or rarely, three) of the standard actions (Sequencing, Selection, Distribution, and Matching) to a set of entities.

The most common Hybrid is Sequencing-Matching. A typical Sequencing-Matching Hybrid game might ask you to schedule six speakers at a conference to six one-hour speaking slots (from 9 am to 2 pm), and then assign each speaker one of two subjects (economic development or trade policy).

Nearly as common as Sequencing-Matching is Distribution-Sequencing. A typical game of this type might ask you to divide six people in a talent competition into either a Dance category or a Singing category, and then rank the competitors in each category.

It is most common to see one Hybrid game in each Logic Games section, although there have been tests with two Hybrid games and tests with none. To determine the type of Hybrid you are faced with, identify the game's action in Step 1 of the Logic Games Method. For example, a game asking you to choose four of six runners, and then assign the four chosen runners to lanes numbered 1 through 4 on a track, would be a Selection-Sequencing Hybrid game.

Mapping Game

A game that provides you with a description of geographical locations and, typically, of the connections among them. Mapping games often ask you to determine the shortest possible routes between two locations or to account for the number of connections required to travel from one location to another. This game type is extremely rare, and as of February 2017, a Mapping game was last seen on PrepTest 40 administered in June 2003.

Process Game

A game that opens with an initial arrangement of entities (e.g., a starting sequence or grouping) and provides rules that describe the processes through which that arrangement can be altered. The questions typically ask you for acceptable arrangements or placements of particular entities after one, two, or three stages in the process. Occasionally, a Process game question might provide information about the arrangement after one, two, or three stages in the process and ask you what must have happened in the earlier stages. This game type is extremely rare, and as of November 2016, a Process game was last seen on PrepTest 16 administered in September 1995. However, there was a Process game on PrepTest 80, administered in December 2016, thus ending a 20-year hiatus.

Game Setups and Deductions

Floater

An entity that is not restricted by any rule or limitation in the game

Blocks of Entities

Two or more entities that are required by rule to be adjacent or separated by a set number of spaces (Sequencing games), to be placed together in the same group (Distribution games), to be matched to the same entity (Matching games), or to be selected or rejected together (Selection games)

Limited Options

Rules or restrictions that force all of a game's acceptable arrangements into two (or occasionally three) patterns

Established Entities

An entity required by rule to be placed in one space or assigned to one particular group throughout the entire game

Number Restrictions

Rules or limitations affecting the number of entities that may be placed into a group or space throughout the game

Duplications

Two or more rules that restrict a common entity. Usually, these rules can be combined to reach additional deductions. For example, if you know that B is placed earlier than A in a sequence and that C is placed earlier than B in that sequence, you can deduce that C is placed earlier than A in the sequence and that there is at least one space (the space occupied by B) between C and A.

Master Sketch

The final sketch derived from the game's setup, rules, and deductions. LSAT experts preserve the Master Sketch for reference as they work through the questions. The Master

Sketch does not include any conditions from New-"If" question stems.

Logic Games Question Types

Acceptability Question

A question in which the correct answer is an acceptable arrangement of all the entities relative to the spaces, groups, or selection criteria in the game. Answer these by using the rules to eliminate answer choices that violate the rules.

Partial Acceptability Question

A question in which the correct answer is an acceptable arrangement of some of the entities relative to some of the spaces, groups, or selection criteria in the game, and in which the arrangement of entities not included in the answer choices could be acceptable to the spaces, groups, or selection criteria not explicitly shown in the answer choices. Answer these the same way you would answer Acceptability questions, by using the rules to eliminate answer choices that explicitly or implicitly violate the rules.

Must Be True/False; Could Be True/False Question

A question in which the correct answer must be true, could be true, could be false, or must be false (depending on the question stem), and in which no additional rules or conditions are provided by the question stem

New-"If" Question

A question in which the stem provides an additional rule, condition, or restriction (applicable only to that question), and then asks what must/could be true/false as a result. LSAT experts typically handle New-"If" questions by copying the Master Sketch, adding the new restriction to the copy, and working out any additional deductions available as a result of the new restriction before evaluating the answer choices.

Rule Substitution Question

A question in which the correct answer is a rule that would have an impact identical to one of the game's original rules on the entities in the game

Rule Change Question

A question in which the stem alters one of the original rules in the game, and then asks what must/could be true/false as a result. LSAT experts typically handle Rule Change questions by reconstructing the game's sketch, but now accounting for the changed rule in place of the original. These questions are rare on recent tests.

Rule Suspension Question

A question in which the stem indicates that you should ignore one of the original rules in the game, and then asks what must/could be true/false as a result. LSAT experts typically handle Rule Suspension questions by reconstructing the game's sketch, but now accounting for the absent rule. These questions are very rare.

Complete and Accurate List Question

A question in which the correct answer is a list of any and all entities that could acceptably appear in a particular space or group, or a list of any and all spaces or groups in which a particular entity could appear

Completely Determine Question

A question in which the correct answer is a condition that would result in exactly one acceptable arrangement for all of the entities in the game

Supply the "If" Question

A question in which the correct answer is a condition that would guarantee a particular result stipulated in the question stem

Minimum/Maximum Question

A question in which the correct answer is the number corresponding to the fewest or greatest number of entities that could be selected (Selection), placed into a particular group (Distribution), or matched to a particular entity (Matching). Often, Minimum/Maximum questions begin with New-"If" conditions.

Earliest/Latest Question

A question in which the correct answer is the earliest or latest position in which an entity may acceptably be placed. Often, Earliest/Latest questions begin with New-"If" conditions.

"How Many" Question

A question in which the correct answer is the exact number of entities that may acceptably be placed into a particular group or space. Often, "How Many" questions begin with New-"If" conditions.

Reading Comprehension
Strategic Reading

Roadmap

The test taker's markup of the passage text in Step 1 (Read the Passage Strategically) of the Reading Comprehension Method. To create helpful Roadmaps, LSAT experts circle or underline Keywords in the passage text and jot down brief, helpful notes or paragraph summaries in the margin of their test booklets.

Keyword(s) in Reading Comprehension

Words in the passage text that reveal the passage structure or the author's point of view and thus help test takers anticipate and research the questions that accompany the passage. LSAT experts pay attention to six categories of Keywords in Reading Comprehension:

Emphasis/Opinion—words that signal that the author finds a detail noteworthy or that the author has positive or negative opinion about a detail; any subjective or evaluative language on the author's part (e.g., *especially, crucial, unfortunately, disappointing, I suggest, it seems likely*)

Contrast—words indicating that the author finds two details or ideas incompatible or that the two details illustrate conflicting points (e.g., *but, yet, despite, on the other hand*)

Logic—words that indicate an argument, either the author's or someone else's (e.g., *thus, therefore, because, it follows that*)

Illustration—words indicating an example offered to clarify or support another point (e.g., *for example, this shows, to illustrate*)

Sequence/Chronology—words showing steps in a process or developments over time (e.g., *traditionally, in the past, today, first, second, finally, earlier, subsequent*)

Continuation—words indicating that a subsequent example or detail supports the same point or illustrates the same idea as the previous example (e.g., *moreover, in addition, also, further, along the same lines*)

Margin Notes

The brief notes or paragraph summaries that the test taker jots down next to the passage in the margin of the test booklet

Big Picture Summaries: Topic/Scope/Purpose/Main Idea

A test taker's mental summary of the passage as a whole made during Step 1 (Read the Passage Strategically) of the Reading Comprehension Method. LSAT experts account for four aspects of the passage in their big picture summaries:

Topic—the overall subject of the passage

Scope—the particular aspect of the Topic that the author focuses on

Purpose—the author's reason or motive for writing the passage (express this as a verb; e.g., *to refute, to outline, to evaluate, to critique*)

Main Idea—the author's conclusion or overall takeaway; if the passage does not contain an explicit conclusion or thesis, you can combine the author's Scope and Purpose to get a good sense of the Main Idea.

Passage Types

Kaplan categorizes Reading Comprehension passages in two ways, by subject matter and by passage structure.

Subject matter categories

In the majority of LSAT Reading Comprehension sections, there is one passage from each of the following subject matter categories:

Humanities—topics from art, music, literature, philosophy, etc.

Natural Science—topics from biology, astronomy, paleontology, physics, etc.

Social Science—topics from anthropology, history, sociology, psychology, etc.

Law—topics from constitutional law, international law, legal education, jurisprudence, etc.

Passage structure categories

The majority of LSAT Reading Comprehension passages correspond to one of the following descriptions. The first categories—Theory/Perspective and Event/Phenomenon—have been the most common on recent LSATs.

Theory/Perspective—The passage focuses on a thinker's theory or perspective on some aspect of the Topic; typically (though not always), the author disagrees and critiques the thinker's perspective and/or defends his own perspective.

Event/Phenomenon—The passage focuses on an event, a breakthrough development, or a problem that has recently arisen; when a solution to the problem is proposed, the author most often agrees with the solution (and that represents the passage's Main Idea).

Biography—The passage discusses something about a notable person; the aspect of the person's life emphasized by the author reflects the Scope of the passage.

Debate—The passage outlines two opposing positions (neither of which is the author's) on some aspect of the Topic; the author may side with one of the positions, may remain neutral, or may critique both. (This structure has been relatively rare on recent LSATs.)

Comparative Reading

A pair of passages (labeled Passage A and Passage B) that stand in place of the typical single passage exactly one time in each Reading Comprehension section administered since June 2007. The paired Comparative Reading passages share the same Topic, but may have different Scopes and Purposes. On most LSAT tests, a majority of the questions accompanying Comparative Reading passages require the test taker to compare or contrast ideas or details from both passages.

Question Strategies

Research Clues

A reference in a Reading Comprehension question stem to a word, phrase, or detail in the passage text, or to a particular line number or paragraph in the passage. LSAT experts recognize five kinds of research clues:

Line Reference—An LSAT expert researches around the referenced lines, looking for Keywords that indicate why the referenced details were included or how they were used by the author.

Paragraph Reference—An LSAT expert consults her passage Roadmap to see the paragraph's Scope and Purpose.

Quoted Text (often accompanied by a line reference)—An LSAT expert checks the context of the quoted term or phrase, asking what the author meant by it in the passage.

Proper Nouns—An LSAT expert checks the context of the person, place, or thing in the passage, asking whether the author made a positive, negative, or neutral evaluation of it and why the author included it in the passage.

Content Clues—These are terms, concepts, or ideas from the passage mentioned in the question stem but not as direct quotes and not accompanied by line references. An LSAT expert knows that content clues almost always refer to something that the author emphasized or about which the author expressed an opinion.

Reading Comp Question Types

Global Question

A question that asks for the Main Idea of the passage or for the author's primary Purpose in writing the passage. Typical question stems:

> Which one of the following most accurately expresses the main point of the passage?

> The primary purpose of the passage is to

Detail Question

A question that asks what the passage explicitly states about a detail. Typical question stems:

> According to the passage, some critics have criticized Gilliam's films on the grounds that

> The passage states that one role of a municipality's comptroller in budget decisions by the city council is to

> The author identifies which one of the following as a commonly held but false preconception?

> The passage contains sufficient information to answer which of the following questions?

Occasionally, the test will ask for a correct answer that contains a detail *not* stated in the passage:

> The author attributes each of the following positions to the Federalists EXCEPT:

Inference Question

A question that asks for a statement that follows from or is based on the passage but that is not necessarily stated explicitly in the passage. Some Inference questions contain research clues. The following are typical Inference question stems containing research clues:

> Based on the passage, the author would be most likely to agree with which one of the following statements about unified field theory?

> The passage suggests which one of the following about the behavior of migratory water fowl?

> Given the information in the passage, to which one of the following would radiocarbon dating techniques likely be applicable?

Other Inference questions lack research clues in the question stem. They may be evaluated using the test taker's Big Picture Summaries, or the answer choices may make it clear that the test taker should research a particular part of the passage text. The following are typical Inference question stems containing research clues:

> It can be inferred from the passage that the author would be most likely to agree that

> Which one of the following statements is most strongly supported by the passage?

Other Reading Comprehension question types categorized as Inference questions are Author's Attitude questions and Vocabulary-in-Context questions.

Logic Function Question

A question that asks why the author included a particular detail or reference in the passage or how the author used a particular detail or reference. Typical question stems:

> The author of the passage mentions declining inner-city populations in the paragraph most likely in order to

> The author's discussion of Rimbaud's travels in the Mediterranean (lines 23–28) functions primarily to

> Which one of the following best expresses the function of the third paragraph in the passage?

Logic Reasoning Question

A question that asks the test taker to apply Logical Reasoning skills in relation to a Reading Comprehension passage. Logic Reasoning questions often mirror Strengthen or Parallel Reasoning questions, and occasionally mirror Method of Argument or Principle questions. Typical question stems:

> Which one of the following, if true, would most strengthen the claim made by the author in the last sentence of the passage (lines 51–55)?

> Which one of the following pairs of proposals is most closely analogous to the pair of studies discussed in the passage?

Author's Attitude Question

A question that asks for the author's opinion or point of view on the subject discussed in the passage or on a detail mentioned in the passage. Since the correct answer may follow from the passage without being explicitly stated in it, some Author's Attitude questions are characterized as a subset of Inference questions. Typical question stems:

> The author's attitude toward the use of DNA evidence in the appeals by convicted felons is most accurately described as

> The author's stance regarding monetarist economic theories can most accurately be described as one of

Vocabulary-in-Context Question

A question that asks how the author uses a word or phrase within the context of the passage. The word or phrase in question is always one with multiple meanings. Since the correct answer follows from its use in the passage, Vocabulary-in-Context questions are characterized as a subset of Inference questions. Typical question stems:

> Which one of the following is closest in meaning to the word "citation" as it used in the second paragraph of the passage (line 18)?

> In context, the word "enlightenment" (line 24) refers to

Wrong Answer Types in RC

Outside the Scope (Out of Scope; Beyond the Scope)

An answer choice containing a statement that is too broad, too narrow, or beyond the purview of the passage

180

An answer choice that directly contradicts what the correct answer must say

Extreme

An answer choice containing language too emphatic (e.g., *all*, *never*, *every*, *none*) to be supported by the passage

Distortion

An answer choice that mentions details or ideas from the passage but mangles or misstates what the author said about those details or ideas

Faulty Use of Detail

An answer choice that accurately states something from the passage but in a manner that incorrectly answers the question

Half-Right/Half-Wrong

An answer choice in which one clause follows from the passage while another clause contradicts or deviates from the passage

Formal Logic Terms

Conditional Statement ("If"-Then Statement)

A statement containing a sufficient clause and a necessary clause. Conditional statements can be described in Formal Logic shorthand as:

> If [sufficient clause] → [necessary clause]

In some explanations, the LSAT expert may refer to the sufficient clause as the statement's "trigger" and to the necessary clause as the statement's result.

For more on how to interpret, describe, and use conditional statements on the LSAT, please refer to "A Note About Formal Logic on the LSAT" in this book's introduction.

Contrapositive

The conditional statement logically equivalent to another conditional statement formed by reversing the order of and negating the terms in the original conditional statement. For example, reversing and negating the terms in this statement:

> *If*   *A*   →   *B*

results in its contrapositive:

> *If*   *~B*   →   *~A*

To form the contrapositive of conditional statements in which either the sufficient clause or the necessary clause has more than one term, you must also change the conjunction *and* to *or*, or vice versa. For example, reversing and negating the terms and changing *and* to *or* in this statement:

> *If*   *M*   →   *O AND P*

results in its contrapositive:

> *If*   *~ O OR ~ P*   →   *~ M*